Jasmina Dimitrieva-Najdanova

Election Standards and their Implementation in Europe

Jasmina Dimitrieva-Najdanova

Election Standards and their Implementation in Europe

LAP LAMBERT Academic Publishing

Impressum / Imprint

Bibliografische Information der Deutschen Nationalbibliothek: Die Deutsche Nationalbibliothek verzeichnet diese Publikation in der Deutschen Nationalbibliografie; detaillierte bibliografische Daten sind im Internet über http://dnb.d-nb.de abrufbar.

Alle in diesem Buch genannten Marken und Produktnamen unterliegen warenzeichen-, marken- oder patentrechtlichem Schutz bzw. sind Warenzeichen oder eingetragene Warenzeichen der jeweiligen Inhaber. Die Wiedergabe von Marken, Produktnamen, Gebrauchsnamen, Handelsnamen, Warenbezeichnungen u.s.w. in diesem Werk berechtigt auch ohne besondere Kennzeichnung nicht zu der Annahme, dass solche Namen im Sinne der Warenzeichen- und Markenschutzgesetzgebung als frei zu betrachten wären und daher von jedermann benutzt werden dürften.

Bibliographic information published by the Deutsche Nationalbibliothek: The Deutsche Nationalbibliothek lists this publication in the Deutsche Nationalbibliografie; detailed bibliographic data are available in the Internet at http://dnb.d-nb.de.

Any brand names and product names mentioned in this book are subject to trademark, brand or patent protection and are trademarks or registered trademarks of their respective holders. The use of brand names, product names, common names, trade names, product descriptions etc. even without a particular marking in this work is in no way to be construed to mean that such names may be regarded as unrestricted in respect of trademark and brand protection legislation and could thus be used by anyone.

Coverbild / Cover image: www.ingimage.com

Verlag / Publisher:
LAP LAMBERT Academic Publishing
ist ein Imprint der / is a trademark of
OmniScriptum GmbH & Co. KG
Heinrich-Böcking-Str. 6-8, 66121 Saarbrücken, Deutschland / Germany
Email: info@lap-publishing.com

Herstellung: siehe letzte Seite /
Printed at: see last page
ISBN: 978-3-659-68338-1

Zugl. / Approved by: Ljubljana, University of Ljubljana, Diss., 2014

Jasmina Dimitrieva, PhD

ELECTION STANDARDS AND THEIR IMPLEMENTATION IN EUROPE

ELECTION STANDARDS AND

THEIR IMPLEMENTATION IN EUROPE

by Jasmina Dimitrieva, PhD

A book dedicated to democracy in Europe, depicting free and fair elections as necessary, yet not sufficient condition of a democratic society

FOREWARDS

>>The book contemplates a measuring tool of elections in Europe based on the simple premise that there is no democracy without free and fair elections, while not all elections represent a key that opens a door for a democratic governance. Substanial respect of the rules set in a comprehensive regulation coupled with a pluralistic democratic millieu may be a guarantee for a free election process and a fair result.

The scientific contribution of this work lies primarily in: a. the original conceptualization of the European election standards, regarding their substance and their legal form (a trilateral agreement to be signed by the election-mandated European organizations); and b. enriching comparative law by a comparison made between election legislation of quite diverse eight countries (Azerbaijan, Belgium, France, Macedonia, Slovenia, Swiss Federation, UK and Ukraine) in light of the conceptualized European standards.

Having in mind that this book tackles the origin, intrinsic elements and sustainability of free and fair elections, as one of the building blocks of representative democracy, but in a unique, way and internationally comparative view, I cordially recommend it as practical tool for practitoners and academics for their contemplated activities and analysis in the election field.

Prof. Dr. Natasha Gaber-Damjanovska
Skopje, 2014

>>Main topic examined in the book are »free and fair elections« in Europe, in particular their philosophical and historic development and their reflection in the international public law. The author examines in a critical way the thesis that although European election standards have already been developed, they are imprecise, fragmented and maybe even confusing for the demand side. I would especially like to emphasise the importance of the proposed new electoral standard in this context, which would make obligatory for the European countries to ensure a meaningful representation of women. Author, among others, examines existing electoral commitments for gender representation put in the context of European standards and subjected to legislative comparative review. Equitable gender representation was further examined under the loop of the non-discrimination principle.

European election standards are not only examined in abstracto, but also in concreto, by showing their application on individual cases by the European Court of Human Rights, as well as by showing their application as a mesuring stick by election observation missions.

The Chapter on EU election standards represents a special contribution to the literature on EU, as it does not only examine election rights granted to the EU citizens, but provides in-depth analysis about the legal effects of the proposed single set of European standards in the legal order of the EU. Another interesting part of the book is connected with the analysis of the legal form in which election European standards should be contained, which tackles in detail the conditions for its legality, not only under the EU but also under the Council of Europe and OSCE rules.

The book is important contribution to the legal scholarship, by exploring in-debt complex issues of the determinants of the power holders in Europe and I cordially recommend this book to the academics and practitioners dealing with elections. The book is written in a clear and simple manner, therefore it representes an enjoyable reading for all holders of active and passive election rights.

Adj. Prof. Dr. Penelopa Gjurcilova
Laos, 2014

CONTENTS

LIST OF ABBREVIATIONS

ACEEO	Association of Central and Eastern European Electoral Officials
CEDAW	Convention on Elimination of All Forms of Discrimination against Women
CIS	Commonwealth of Independent States
CoE	Council of Europe
CLRAE	Congress of Local and Regional Democracy
CM	Committee of Ministers of CoE
EB	Electoral Board
ECHR	European Convention on Human Rights
ECtHR	European Court of Human Rights
EMB	Electoral Management Body
EP	European Parliament
EU	European Union
GRECO	Group of States against Corruption
HRC	Human Rights Committee
ICCPR	International Covenant on Civil and Political Rights
ICERD	International Convention on Elimination of Racial Discrimination
ICRPD	International Convention on the Rights of the Persons with Disabilities
ICESC	International Covenant on Economic, Social and Cultural Rights
IPU	International Parliamentary Union
ODIHR	Office for Democratic Institutions and Human Rights
ToL	Treaty of Lisbon
SC	Security Council
SEC	State Electoral Commission
SG	Secretary-General
UDHR	Universal Declaration of Human Rights
UN	United Nations
VC	Venice Commission
VL	Voters' List

I. INTRODUCTION

The development of human rights law has engaged the responsibility of states for the protection of human rights, as well as for the creation of conditions for their enjoyment by citizens. In the parts of Europe with democratic systems (after the World War II) this trend has been nurtured by the CoE since its inception in 1949. But, for the parts of Europe with socialistic political systems, the main impetus for the protection of human rights came with the collapse of the Berlin Wall, which demonstrated that citizens will always find a way to request and fulfill their right to live in a free society and to elect their representatives. The democratization of the continent has been further supported by the European Union's enlargement process, which requires a democratic governance and human rights protection. Nowadays, nobody can contest that the right to participate in public affairs and its intrinsic component, election rights, represent a fundamental human right. They are foreseen in major international instruments, which oblige the states to afford their protection and to create conditions for their free enjoyment by the people.

Democratic governance is not a new invention. Its roots are traced back to ancient times. Although Athenian style of governance is celebrated as an archetype of democracy, political rights there were non-existent for females, slaves and free persons, whose parents were not citizens. From ancient philosophers, Aristotle considered democracy one of the worst political systems as it was in favor of the rulers (the people who were poor) and not in favor of the common good, thus boosting political instability and irrationality.[1] Plato in "The Republic" thought that democracy ran the risk of degenerating into a tyranny as the majority was composed of independent workers who did not own much and did not conduct public affairs, thus could be easily manipulated.

In Rome, democracy was thought of in terms of republic, which meant freedom from the arbitrary power of tyrants in conjunction with the right of the citizens to conduct public affairs through representation in government. Women, slaves and a large foreign population were excluded from the electorate. In the Middle Ages the belief that royal right to rule

---

[1] Miller, The Blackwell Encyclopedia of Political Thought (Macedonian translation, published by MI-AN) (2002) p. 94.

I. Introduction

derived from God was challenged by the theory of the social contract, which placed the origin of sovereignty in individuals with natural rights and freedoms.[2]

The limitation of power via written constitution, was finally established in the 18th century by the Constitution of the United States, which provided for a government elected by white male owners of property, and protected civil rights and liberties. In Europe, the idea that the origin of sovereignty was the people, and that nobody could govern without direct authorization from the people, was enshrined in the 1789 French Declaration of the Rights of the Man and of the Citizen adopted by the National Assembly. In the 19th century there was a trend towards more and more groups of citizens, including persons who were economically dependent upon others and working for others,[3] gaining formal voting rights. The social turbulences aimed at limiting the political arbitrariness went hand in hand with the refreshing changes in the political and legal scholarship.

In particular, Kant's "contractus originarius" bound the legislator to have all its laws originating from the collective will of the people, or else they would have the right to disobey him. In the 19th century, liberal thinkers such as Alexis de Tocqueville considered that the principle of presidential re-eligibility encouraged the corrupting influence of power, and thus had to be limited. Jeremy Bentham, a leading figure of utilitarianism considered that each literate individual should have the right to vote for a representative. The general right to vote was further supported by James Mill, who named the phenomenon as "the big discovery of modern times". Karl Marx considered that the universal right to vote would be a revolutionary measure, resulting in the superiority of the working class.[4] For anarchists, elections were used to trick the masses to support one or another member of the ruling class.[5] The twentieth century was marked with the Russian October revolution and the Nazi dictatorship. The end of WWII brought an end to fascism and to the possibility of a democratic reversal in society. However, dictatorships in East and Southern Europe that existed at that time left little space for democracy. Despite the ideological division between

---

[2] Miller, The Blackwell Encyclopedia of Political Thought (Macedonian translation, published by MI-AN) (2002) pp. 94, 379.
[3] Ibid, p. 80.
[4] Ishay, The Human Rights Reader: major political essays and documents from the Bible to the present, (Macedonian translation, published by MI-AN) (1997) p. 184.
[5] Miller, The Blackwell Encyclopedia of Political Thought (Macedonian translation, published by MI-AN) (2002) pp. 21-22.

I. Introduction

East and West, the Universal Declaration of Human Rights and the Covenant on Civil and Political Rights were approved in 1948 and 1966 respectively, which contained provisions stipulating universal, periodic, secret and equal suffrage. The trend towards democracy and elections with multi-party choice started in the 1990s with the end of the cold war, the disintegration of the Soviet Union and former Yugoslavia.

In the 20th and 21st centuries, elections remain the core feature of democracy. They continued to challenge authors to search for solutions to the contemporary political problems. Robert A. Dahl sketched out a theory about modern democracy, the so-called "polyarchy". He considered that democratic theory was at a minimum concerned with the processes by which ordinary citizens exerted a high level of control over leaders.[6] Consensual democracy was explored by Lijphard[7] using the Netherlands as a model with its plural and progressive society. The basic premise is that political representation of different social groups in fragmented societies should govern the country by consensus.

More specifically on election rights' theories, Walter James Shepard set out five conflicting theories of voting rights. Under the "Vested Privilege Theory", voting rights were considered a privilege for adults who owned property of a certain value. Under the "Natural Rights Theory" the rights to vote and to stand for elections with no limitations were considered a natural right of all human beings. Under the "Government Function Theory", the voters performed a public government office, and thus it was perfectly acceptable to put certain limitations on voting rights and to disenfranchise criminals, paupers and the insane in order to make the electorate "a more efficient organ of government". Under the "Ethical Theory" voting rights were considered the highest form of political expression which should enjoy the same protection as the rights of expression and association. Under the "Theory of Political Equality", everyone was permitted to vote on an equal basis, so the outcome of the elections had to be protected, i.e., the candidate receiving more votes than any other had to receive the office.

---

[6] Dahl, A Preface to Democratic Theory (1956, 1984, 2006) pp. xviii, 3 and 132.
[7] Lijphart, Patterns of Democracy (Serbian translation, published by Sluzbeni List SCG Beograd) (1999).

I. Introduction

The ideas of justice, equality and freedom which emerged in the era of enlightenment as well as natural law theories inspired changes in human society and raised consciousness regarding political freedoms and election rights. They became subject of international concern, since elections facilitate stability, peace and security not only at a national, but also at an international level. Full protection of human rights and enjoyment of democracy is thought to help prevention of intra-state violence and inter-state conflicts, thus contributing to worldwide peace and security. Ballots are replacing the bullets to select who will govern countries.[8]

In the contemporary world, there are not just opportunities for democracy, but there are also challenges to it. Terrorism, wars, environmental and technological changes, poverty, lack of energy, demographic trends all represent challenges for states. Such problems might contribute governing power to fall in the hands of individuals and governments who are corrupt, who defraud the electoral process, or who restrict and manipulate basic freedoms.

Although periodical fair and free elections with well-protected election rights lie at the heart of democracy, they must not become a synonym for democracy. They are but a part of the wider right to participate in public affairs, which besides election rights, guarantees political association, participation in political decision-making and in the formulation of public policies and their implementation, as well as equal access for the citizens not only to elected, but also to administrative offices at all levels of government. It further encompasses the right to be directly consulted through referendums, the right to peaceful assembly, and the right to bring citizen's initiatives for regulating some issues of public importance when provided for by law.[9]

Both ICCPR and ECHR allow for restriction of freedom of expression and freedom of association also in political context, because of specified reasons such as national security, protection of the rights and reputation of others, and protection of morals provided that they are set out by law and necessary. However, these exceptions must be balanced well with the rights of individuals. On one hand, if the electorate is not fully informed by free media, it would be impossible to guarantee that elections would reflect the will of people. On the other

---

[8] Paraphrasing Abraham Lincoln: "Ballots are the rightful and peaceful successors to bullets".
[9] OSCE/ODIHR, OSCE Human Dimension Commitments, Volume 1 Thematic Compilation (2005) pp. 75, 80 at <http:/www.osce.org>; ICCPR Article 25.

I. Introduction

hand, the state must regulate activities like hate speech, and prohibit discrimination in order to ensure a political environment which is free of intimidation. The state must also protect public demonstrations and rallies as an effective mechanism for the dissemination of political information. The right to privacy, which protects individuals from unlawful wire-tapping and letter-opening must be safeguarded as unlawful interference with this right may easily lead to spying on members of the opposition or denying them access to public administrative offices. At any rate, the enjoyment of the right to participate in public affairs and other political rights must be protected, in order not to remain at a level of philosophical and moral concept.

Furthermore, according to the ICCPR and ICESC all peoples have the right, in full freedom, to determine their internal and external political status when and as they wish in a democratic way without external interference, and to pursue as they wish their political, economic, social and cultural development. On balance, the right to self-determination cannot run counter to the integrity of a state territory, as guaranteed by public international law.

The right to participate in government and connected rights provide the complex mosaic which have summoned a school of thought, which speaks about the right to democratic governance in the international system. According to the prominent scholars Fox and Franck, if the right to political participation is to be effective, the international level should have the power to prescribe more detailed legally-binding standards regarding how participation should be effectuated and should monitor their compliance. Within this line of thought, Roth developed a theory concerning the emergence of a norm of government illegitimacy. In particular, he argues that it cannot be expected for a regime to be recognized with sovereign authority under international law only on the basis that it holds power.[10] It remains to be seen how and when the international community can challenge legitimacy of allegedly freely elected candidates and governments, since in these cases it might appear that sovereignty does not reside in the people of the country, but in international and regional organizations.

Empirical evidence suggest that electoral violations and impunity for those who commit them continue to persist in Europe. It could equally be said that, in some instances, electoral processes have accomplished little more than to allow voters to select from among the parties

---

[10] Governmental Illegitimacy in International Law (2000) pp. 1-3.

dominated by the economic and social elite, without any public impact on policy-making. Elections still yield outcomes that can be characterized as undemocratic and appear to give carte blanche to the majority for oppressing the minority. This is especially true for partially or incompletely consolidated democracies, and thus lowers public confidence in democratic institutions.

A positive and a negative correlation exists between political instability and violence on one side, and elections on the other side. Elections are in opposition to an armed conflict, as it is inconceivable to hold free and fair elections under war conditions. However, they are always held after a peace truce is signed between the parties of a conflict. Elections are generally thought of contributing to the stability of a country. Nevertheless, they can also cause the instability, e.g., in case of non-acceptance of election results by the war lords.[11] The role of elections is even more gaining in importance in these days of globalization and European integration, but also of security threats, which might result in the reduction of basic freedoms and promote aggressive behavior.

Considering the above, the authority to ensure that safeguards for free and fair elections are in place is endowed upon international organizations and human rights instruments. European election rules and principles are set out in all major international human rights instruments, for example, the ECHR, the Code of Good Practice in Electoral Matters, the OSCE Commitments and the Charter of Local Self Government. These instruments aim to ensure the protection of the election rights of the people in the European corner of the world, from any act or omission of a state body/official, whose actions are attributable to the state.[12] OSCE, CoE, EU have a mandate to complement electoral activities of the states in Europe by assessing electoral laws in light of international election standards, by conducting election observation and by adjudicating individual election-related complaints.

---

[11] See the case of Haiti (the SC Resolution no. 948 (1994)) as well as the cases of Angola (the SC Resolutions 747 (1992) and 785 (1992)) and Burma - Union of Myanmar (the SC Resolutions nos. 46/132 (1991) 47/144 (1993) 18/150 (1994) 49/197 (1995) 50/194 (1996) 51/117 (1996) 52/137 (1998) 53/162 (1999) 54/186 (2000) 55/112 (2001) 56/231 (2002) 57/231 (2003) 58/247 (2004) 59/263 (2005) 60/23 (2006)).
[12] The 2001 Articles on Responsibility of States for Internationally Wrongful Acts (ARSIWA) adopted by the International Law Commission at its 53rd session, on 3 August 2001, Articles 3, 4 and 12. The UN General Assembly took note of the Articles by its Resolution A/Res/56/83 (2002), A/56/49(Vol. I)/Corr.4.

I. Introduction

It is the task of the UN and its Security Council to preserve global peace and security. This objective is kept in mind in their election-related activities, which take place in very difficult conditions. Verification of elections may be also linked with authorization of the use of force by the Security Council, especially in case of humanitarian catastrophe, e.g., Haiti and Angola. Therefore, election observation, monitoring, verification and supervision must be perceived as neutral. Election observers must be highly competent in order to notice even the more sophisticated ways of tampering with elections and be sure that the results reflect the voters' will. So, no errors are allowed from international observation missions.

Nevertheless, problems appear with respect to this type of election assessment in case of violence and political unrest. Firstly, since these missions are costly, there might be a lack of funds to conduct them, to do that on a larger scale, or to ensure a follow-up mission or action, as in some instances democratic elections do not necessarily restore stability and peace in the country concerned. Secondly, there might be a lack of time for proper preparation of the mission and/or a lack of knowledge of the political context, election law and procedures of the country concerned. There might be also a lack of capacity to properly follow all phases of the elections and not only election day. Thirdly, the election assessment missions take place in very difficult political circumstances, with significant ramifications for the region. Therefore, missions might sometime give a better evaluation of the elections than deserved in order to avoid destabilizing the country concerned.[13]

The UN conducts fewer and fewer election observation missions. It focuses its energies on providing electoral technical assistance instead. With the changes in the regime introduced by the "Arab spring" since 2011, there was a high demand for electoral assistance from Tunisia, Libya and Egypt, as well as from Yemen (the Middle East). Although national authorities conducted the elections, the UN bodies and missions provided continuous support to ensure a peaceful transition of power to a new set of politicians. As for Europe, the observation of elections is done primarily by the OSCE. This organization can also substantially help a country to conduct free and fair elections following a civil war or political and security tensions, as shown by the examples of Bosnia and Herzegovina and Kosovo.

---

[13] Beyond Intractability, Braham (2004) p. 3 at <http://www.beyondintractability.org>.

I. Introduction

*

*   *

In short, the book examines the following thesis:

1) European standards in the election field may be deduced from the treaties and political commitments of the three European organizations (CoE, OSCE and EU) that have prescribed criteria for holding periodic free and fair elections. However, these standards are imprecise, with varying degrees of legal value and do not fully ensure their sustainability.

2) Free and fair elections, the minimalist concept of democracy, represent a challenge for a number of states in Europe. Therefore, the European organizations, with the aim of maximizing their electoral support efforts, should: i) elaborate uniform European standards in the election field - a common denominator for holding periodic free and fair elections; and ii) establish a coordinative Electoral Secretariat within the OSCE, mandated to assist the states with their electoral reforms.

Primary research methods encompass legal analysis, analogy, comparison and desk research. Interviews with sixteen electoral experts and officials from OSCE/ODIHR, the CoE (Parliamentary Assembly, CLRAE and Venice Commission), UNDP, Slovenia and Macedonia provide institutional and national perceptions relating to the afore-mentioned issues.

II. UNIVERSALITY OF FREE AND FAIR ELECTIONS

1. The Paradigm of "Free and Fair Elections"

Since not every election leads to democratic governance, the standard of "free and fair elections" must capture its minimal requirements in the election field. Due to its importance as an actual measurement of an election, the meaning of the "free and fair elections" has been subject of scientific and pragmatic examinations. For some authors there is no fixed, universal standard of electoral competition that denotes "free and fair elections", as the elections must be assessed from the perspective of whether or not they contribute towards a consolidation of democracy.[14] Other author believes that international law provides only: "… the standard to be achieved, namely that the election produces an outcome which expresses the will of the people".[15]

The constituent part "free" of the "free and fair elections" standard ensures guarantees for the universal active and passive election rights, where only reasonable restrictions are allowed, (age, nationality requirement, conviction for a serious crime). The constituent part "fairness" rests on the tenet of equal opportunities for all participants in the competitive electoral process. All voters have equal power to vote, electoral districts are established on an equitable basis, and the election results accurately reflect the will of the people living in that territory. Effective and adequate remedies guard against abuse of public funds, political censorship and unequal access to media.

The standard "free and fair elections" applies not only to election day, but to the whole electoral cycle: a pre-election phase, an election day and a post-election phase. Each of these phases has various elements: legal framework and electoral system; electoral administration, budgeting and planning; voters' education, information, registration; nomination of candidates; electoral campaign; election day; verification of results; and peaceful transfer of

---

[14] Elklit, Svensson, The Rise of Election Monitoring: What makes elections free and fair? (1997) pp. 35-36, 38-39, 41 and 43.
[15] Goodwin-Gill, Free and Fair Elections (2006) p. 80.

power.[16] The electoral cycle connotes the regularity of elections. They should be held periodically (not more than 7 years depending on the type of election)[17] in order to reflect the will of the people. Therefore, it is also necessary to deduce the specific election standards pertaining to the electoral system and law, voters, candidates, electoral campaign, media, financing, counting and tabulation, allocation of mandates and election observation. All the specific standards from a particular field feed into the overall standard of "free and fair elections" in a systematic and coherent way.

2. Emerging Electoral Standard of Meaningful Representation

The democratic ideas came as a response to the secretive and elitist decision-making, where the people did not have any say regarding the decisions that affected them. In view of the democratic developments worldwide that go hand in hand with a greater inclusion of women and minorities, with the requirements for more just electoral systems and greater accountability of the government, the electoral outcome requiring a meaningful representation is emerging as an electoral standard. It provides a nexus between the voters, their specific interests and their representation in the decision-making via the electoral system. Thus, the electoral system plays primary role regarding the number of votes needed and procedures applied in order to win an electoral office.

This emerging standard of electoral outcome covers a bundle of particles, as follows:
First, the meaningful representation is achieved when there is a high turnout of voters who actually vote. Second, the electoral system accurately reflects the voters' preferences, with the least possible wasted votes. It follows, that the electoral system chosen must accurately translate casted votes into the seats to the extent possible. Therefore, high electoral thresholds must be avoided. While it is states' prerogative to choose their own electoral systems, a legitimate debate is on-going about how to ensure representativeness, i.e., that the votes won by candidates ensure proportional seats, with the smallest possible distortion. Current level of knowledge indicates that proportional electoral system(s) ensure better representativeness than first-past-the post. The international standards do not specify the type of electoral system. Nevertheless, the states should make an effort to allow the widest possible

---

[16] EC-UNDP, Operational Guidelines for the Implementation of an Electoral Assistance Project (2006).
[17] CoE, Code of Good Practice in Electoral Matters, p. 24.

representation of the people leaving in their territories as a democratic value. The electoral systems should not be considered carved in stone; they can also change in order to suit best the realities on the ground. An innovative approach towards electoral systems is also a powerful instrument to end and mitigate hostilities and conflicts, as they can result in acceptance of the results, and in power-sharing arrangements, instead of "winners take all". Evenmore so, that in the latter case, the opposition may find itself weakened for the next elections and unable effectively to perform its function, which is an indispensible condition for democracy.

The reserved seats for minority communities or gender quotas that correct historico-social inequalities vis-à-vis decision-making, represent the third element in this regard. The fourth element connotes that the elected representatives have sufficient power to influence the decision-making, and can hold the government accountable, which is a question that falls to be examined under political systems. The standard of meaningful representation goes hand in hand with a sustainability of free and fair elections.

3. Universal Instruments as a Source of European Election Standards

The UN instruments that guarantee election rights must not be ignored when the content of the European standards in the election field is analyzed, as most of the European countries have ratified them, and thus are legally bound to abide by them. The International Bill of Human Rights has enunciated election rights as one of the pillars of the right to participate in public affairs. Article 21 of the UDHR sets out the participatory process, in which free, fair, regular and universal elections with secret and equal suffrage represent an important segment. Actually, the participatory right as defined herein opened the door for challenging a government's established hold on power, if it has not been perceived as legitimate and in accordance with international standards.

The UDHR's wording regarding elections, which lies at the core of democratic government, is also found in the 1966 ICCPR (Article 25 (b)). Both, the UDHR and ICCPR represent a source not only of international, but also of the European standards in the election field. The former serves as an expression of a universal intent about the end state of the human condition in an ideal world. The latter has been ratified by the European states, and has thus become part of their internal legal order.

The HRC, the ICCPR's enforcement mechanism, has shed light on the electoral criteria. Its General Comment no. 25 which clarifies the scope and content of this article and serves as a guideline for the preparation of country reports. On the general note, election rights are individual and not collective rights. Each individual citizen must have effective opportunity to enjoy these rights, regardless whether he has been born or naturalized in the respective country. Any restrictions on active and passive election rights based on property requirements, disability, extensive residence, party membership, ethnicity, religion, literacy requirement cannot be accepted as reasonable restrictions. In conclusion, restrictions must not be arbitrary, i.e., they must be lawful and based on objective and reasonable criteria, e.g., persons of older age are required to execute some public functions.

Regarding individual communications, the following examples illustrate the requirements for objective and reasonable restrictions:
In the case *No. 314/1988* against Zaire, the HRC concluded that prohibiting the leading opposition figure to take part in an election campaign, based on the fact that he was a member of political party other than the one officially recognized, amounted to an unreasonable restriction. In the communication *No. 500/1992* against the Netherlands, where a policemen elected to local council was not allowed to occupy the office, the HRC found no violation, as it held that since Article 25 rights are not absolute, they cannot be violated as long as the restriction was objective and not discriminatory, and in the instant case there was a conflict of interest. The communication *No. 884/1999* against Latvia concerned the refusal by State party authorities to let an individual stand for the local elections on the basis of a language proficiency test, which according to HRC did not observe the requirement of fairness. In case *No. 1047/2002* against Belarus, the author did not have any effective and impartial remedy to challenge the ruling of the Central Election Commission rejecting his candidacy, as decided by HRC. In the communication *No. 1134/2002* against Cameroon, the HRC found a violation when a person with a different political affiliating from the ruling party was deprived of liberty and deleted from electoral rolls. In the case *No. 1553/2007* against Belarus, the HRC established a breach as the domestic courts seized the campaign material of an opposition

presidential candidate, thereby violating the obligation to ensure the free flow of information about political and public issue by way of publishing political materials and electoral canvassing.

As it transpires from the above, the elections conducted in line with ICCPR must be:

1) Free and universal i.e., the citizens must have their right and opportunity to stand for office and vote of their own choosing ensured with no discrimination. There must be no intimidations or other kinds of pressure imposed on political activists or voters.

2) Fair i.e., which is inconceivable without the equality of the vote principle, requiring that every registered voter has an equal voting power: the same number of votes, and electoral precincts in line with such a principle. Unreasonably high fees or conflicts of interest are incompatible with this principle.

3) Regular i.e., the period between elections must reflect the will of the people and must be determined by law, elections must not be canceled for an indefinite period, and even in case of an emergency situation, the country must ensure holding of new elections.

4) Secret, i.e., any waiver of secrecy is incompatible with ICCPR. The assistance of voters e.g., blind, illiterate, must be impartial and they must be fully informed of their rights.

5. Lawful i.e., conducted with full observance of legal requirements. Effective legal remedies by impartial bodies must be available for any kind of violations of electoral rights; electoral campaigns financing must be transparent; the election result must be implemented.

It is apparent from the Annual Reports of the HRC to the General Assembly that the principles and "philosophy" or the "policy" behind the work of the HRC remains constant, i.e., its interest in the promotion of the rights of political participation of women and minorities, the values of political pluralism, and the universality of election rights and their interdependence with other ICCPR rights, like freedom of association or the right to peaceful assembly.

From other election-related UN Instruments, CEDAW is worth mentioning, which is devoted to the protection of women's rights. Its Article 7 requires from the ratifying states to put in place temporary measures to promote the participation of women in the political decision-making. However, the responsibility to appoint women in advisory and other high positions does not rest solely with the states by way of taking different measures to this effect, but also with political parties who should include women on the candidates' lists where they have likelihood of electoral success.[18] Nevertheless, women still face difficulties when exercising election rights and the number of elected women continues to be low. The requirement for equality of men and women in political decision-making clearly goes not only to the very heart of every domestic political system, but also of tradition, religion and social and family values. Therefore, a true change requires a change of a mind-set.

Participation in public affairs, also by way of elections, has been treated in other specific human rights' documents -the ICERD and the ICRPD. The former foresees an obligation for the ratifying states to guarantee to everyone political rights, in particular active and passive election rights without any form of discrimination.[19] As reckoned by European Commission, if none of the representatives of a particular group is nominated to run in elections due to his/her national affiliation or gender, it is of little use that he or she is granted passive election right. Many governments still do not wish to discuss racial discrimination and deny its existence, considering this topic a taboo. The latter UN document has recognized election rights of persons with mental and physical impairments as universal human rights' concerns. They should participate on an equal basis with others in elections, both as candidates and voters. For example, voters with physical impairments are effectively disfranchised when a polling station is physically inaccessible. Persons with disabilities must also enjoy the right to effectively take office once elected and perform all other public functions with the appropriate assistance. When Article 1, which covers persons with a long-term mental disability, and Article 29 of the Convention setting out political and election rights are read in conjunction, it follows that the CRPD gives rights to people with long-term psychological disorders to vote and stand for elections. Therefore, CRPD has a profound impact on the qualifications for voters and candidates.

---

[18] Steiner, Alston, International Human Rights in Context, Law, Politics, Morals (2nd edition) (2000) pp. 196-199.
[19] Racial discrimination is defined as: any distinction, exclusion, restriction or preference based on race, color, descent or national or ethnic origin which has the purpose or effect of nullifying or impairing the recognition, enjoyment or exercise, on an equal footing, of human rights and fundamental freedoms in the political, economic, social, cultural or any other field of public life.

II. Universality of free and fair elections

Although a number of UN documents serve as a source of the overall international election standard of "free and fair elections", there is no single UN document that sets out all electoral standards. The issue arises as to whether or not the present mosaic of binding (and non-binding) UN documents provides a sufficient legal framework for powerful implementation of the election standards. Alternatively, it may be that the lack of a detailed and coherent UN document on election standards allows the states to evade international election principles. The lack of unified and precise election standards might also result in the UN assessments and assistance relying mostly on the comparative election standards or on the standards belonging to another international organization.

It has been argued that since the main international election standards have been foreseen and similarly defined in all relevant international documents and since there is sufficient state practice in this respect, they have become a part of customary international law, thereby obligatory for states when they hold elections. If that were the case, a hypothetical legally-binding treaty on elections would serve the purpose of systematization of the election standards. It can be equally argued that since elections are considered internal affairs and there is no prescribed form of democracy, there is no place for a detailed document regardless of whether it is or is not legally-binding, since it is within the states' realm to regulate how the individuals will participate in public affairs and make decisions about their government depending on history and traditions. It is also questionable whether a legally-binding detailed treaty on election standards, prepared under UN auspices is needed in the European context, knowing that there are a number of European documents regulating this area. In view of different social and political realities in the world, a legally-binding electoral document might have value for the UN member states that struggle with big electoral challenges. However, such a document might be counterproductive in the European region, for the following reason: it may be used as a means to lower the election standards applicable in Europe, which have already been set out in the European instruments examined herein.

III. EUROPEAN REGIONAL ORGANIZATIONS DEVELOPING STANDARDS IN THE ELECTION FIELD

The European electoral heritage has inspired further development of electoral commitments for increased protection of the rights of the citizens in the election arena.[20] The European electoral commitments are set out in a number of international documents prepared under the auspices of European organizations (the CoE, the OSCE and the EU). Some of the instruments like the ECHR and the Charter of Local Self Government are legally-binding. Others, like the OSCE commitments and the Code of Good Practice in Electoral Matters are not legally-binding. Some of the instruments are applicable only with respect to a particular type of election, or are lacking detail.

In view of the abundance of sources of election standards, and considering the risk of disparities among them, the question arises as to the reasons for the absence of a single legally-binding instrument in which election standards are codified. Alternatively, are European standards sufficiently developed and precise to provide good basis for conducting free and fair elections, and thus no need arises for election treaty? Addressing the gap in knowledge warrants analysis of election-related instruments of the three European organizations.

1. Council of Europe

CoE instruments range from legally-binding treaties, which contain standards only for a particular type of an election to a detailed catalogue of election standards, but with no binding force. In view of the multiple CoE sources from which the election standards are derived and the relevant enforcement bodies, the instruments tackled in this chapter can be perceived as a single CoE electoral rights protection mechanism.

---

[20] CoE, Code of Good Practices in Electoral Matters, Adopted Guidelines and Draft Explanatory Report, European Commission for Democracy Through Law (CDL-EL (2002) 5) section I.5.

1.1. Election of Legislature: The European Convention on Human Rights

The ECHR is, *par excellence,* a standard-setting instrument at the European level. It binds all members of the CoE, since any country aspiring to be its member must ratify it. Ratifying states are left with a certain margin of appreciation due to their sovereignty,[21] but in no way should the rights and freedoms guaranteed by the ECHR be impinged to the extent to impede their very essence. The provisions of the ECHR are interpreted in light of its object and purpose. This means that the ECtHR interprets the ECHR while taking into consideration important concepts defined in its Preamble like "effective political democracy" and "democratic society". It further takes into consideration the relationship that exists between various human rights and freedoms, and thus looks at the ECHR as a whole.

The wording of Article 3, Protocol no. 1 of ECHR, which requires elections to be conducted under the conditions which allow for free expression of the will of the people, underlines the need for enjoyment of other civil and political rights. This inter linkage with other ECHR rights is underscored, considering that any interference with election rights must be compatible with the object and purpose of Article 3, Protocol no. 1 of the ECHR.[22] The ECtHR subjects to closer scrutiny the cases where the freedom of expression of the politicians is at stake,[23] because politicians also bear greater responsibility to society. This increased responsibility is due to the influence that politicians have over the masses, the relatively greater ease with which they could mobilize the people to commit violent acts.[24]

In electoral context, the non-discrimination principle set out in ECHR is applied in the nomination of the candidates, during the electoral campaign, in the composition of the electoral administration and during the voting, counting and tallying processes. The right to effective remedy granted by ECHR is indispensable for the resolution of electoral disputes, since it is the judiciary that is charged with safeguarding the rule of law before, during and after elections. An independent judiciary does not replace the functioning of independent

---

[21] Van Dijk, Van Hoof, Theory and Practice of the European Convention on Human Rights (1998), pp. 82-95.
[22] Ibid, pp. 72-73.
[23] See on the necessity of interference, the case of *Rufi Osmani v. Macedonia*, Application no. 50841/99, Final Decision of 11 October 2001.
[24] Harris, Boyle, Warbrick, Law of the European Convention on Human Rights (1995) pp. 12-16.

electoral bodies, but acts complimentary to them by allowing for peaceful dispute resolution and by protecting candidates and voters from any kind of intimidation and denigration.[25]

In this context, it is worth noting that in a number of cases the ECtHR declared the complaints under Article 6 about the unfairness of judicial proceedings inadmissible, holding that political rights, and not civil rights were at stake. The ECtHR gave no consideration to the fact that Article 6 is applicable when an administrative decision is challenged,[26] and that in many European countries electoral disputes are processed in accordance with the administrative procedure. Nonetheless, through its decisions in several cases against Azerbaijan[27] under ECHR Article 3, Protocol no. 1, the ECtHR seems to have implicitly extended a number of "fair trial" safeguards to electoral arena, since it requires a thorough and effective investigation and impartial and objective examination of election-related cases by an impartial electoral administration.

(i) Article 3 of Protocol no. 1 to the ECHR

Whereas all member states of the CoE are parties to the ECHR, not all of them are a party to its Protocol no. 1, which contains election guarantees. Switzerland and Monaco have not ratified Protocol no. 1. It can only be speculated why these two countries, one of which is a model democracy, still have not ratified the Protocol, which contains the minimal criteria for "free and fair" elections of the legislature. Regarding Monaco, a constitutional monarchy, the reason may be found in the division of the legislative power that exists between the National Council (directly elected legislative body) and the prince.[28] The fear that this delicate balance may be affected by Article 3 of Protocol no. 1 of the ECHR, may be the reason for a lack of adherence to the Protocol. As to Switzerland, the speculations focus on its specific political system. Namely, the Swiss confederation is based on the principle of subsidiarity, and a distribution of the legislative powers between the federal assembly and the cantonal assemblies. Since the cantons have legislative powers, Article 3 of Protocol no. 1 of the ECHR would also apply to them. However, the representatives of the cantonal legislative bodies are elected in different manners, with each canton having its own rules regarding

---

[25] Harris, Boyle, Warbrick, Law of the European Convention on Human Rights (1995) pp. 163-196.
[26] Van Dijk, Hoof, Theory and Practice of the European Convention on Human Rights (1998) p. 397.
[27] For example, *Namat Aliyev v. Azerbaijan.*
[28] Article 4 of the 1962 Constitution of the Principality of Monaco.

various aspects of elections. Moreover, the federal assembly elections are governed by cantonal laws regarding the media, electoral administration and other specific segments, with the federal legislation only regulating general electoral principles.[29] It follows that a lack of uniform rules might be hypothetically perceived as unequal treatment of the citizens under the ECHR. If a complaint for a lack of equal treatment would be successful, the Swiss cantons would have to harmonize their electoral systems, thus re-shaping the Swiss political landscape.

Article 3 of Protocol no. 1[30] does not explicitly protect other components of the right to participate in public affairs, such as access to civil service on an equal basis, consultation about legislative projects,[31] or control of government by the legislature.[32] It does not cover referendums either.

Under ECHR indirect democracy is derogable. If the derogation continues beyond necessity for a long time, the question arises if other ECHR provisions can be enjoyed effectively under such circumstances.[33] In such a case, one could not speak about a democratic society, which is the essential object of protection afforded by the ECHR.

The structure of Article 3 of P-1 contains nine determinants, as follows:
First, in comparison to other substantive ECHR articles where an individual is expressly the holder of the right prescribed, this article is explicitly directed to the high contracting parties. The ambiguity of the language was resolved by giving the individuals and political parties the right to petition for protection of their active and passive election rights.
The ECtHR's liberal approach vis-à-vis the procedure has opened a door to invoke the protection of the electoral rights. Had the ECtHR taken a conservative approach, the protection of the electoral rights would have been ineffective, taking into consideration that – until now there has not been a single inter-state application complaining about rigged

---

[29] OSCE/ODIHR, Election Assessment Report on Swiss 2011 Federal Assembly Elections, pp. 1-4.
[30] It reads as follows: "The High Contracting Parties undertake to hold free elections at reasonable intervals by secret ballot, under conditions which will ensure the free expression of the opinion of the people in the choice of the legislature".
[31] Van Dijk, Hoof, Theory and Practice of the European Convention on Human Rights (1998) pp. 658-659.
[32] Harris, Boyle, Warbrick, Law of the European Convention on Human Rights (1995) p. 554.
[33] The Greek case, 12 YB 1 179-180 1969.

elections. The lack of inter-state applications (despite the re-occurring electoral violations) may be due to the States' cautious approach when the political rights are at stake, but also to the lack of the ECtHR's adequate remedial powers regarding rigged elections.

Second, the language of the respective article reads "people" and not "citizens". Therefore, it is the choice of the state whether or not to allow the non-citizens to vote or stand for elections, as there is no clear definition which categories are included in the definition of "people". However, it should be born in mind that Article 1 of the ECHR stipulates that all its rights are guaranteed to everyone within the jurisdiction of the ratifying states.

Third, the ratifying states must hold elections in line with the requirements in the Preamble for building and maintaining effective democracy.

Fourth, ECHR guarantees apply only for the election of legislature. The term "legislature" has been subject of extensive case-law with the ECtHR again taking a liberal approach, thus broadening the ambit of admissibility of Article 3 of Protocol no. 1 to the ECHR.

The fifth, sixth and seventh determinants are reflected in the electoral requirements of the CoE countries. The elections must be free, periodic and secret, thus indicating the most significant electoral principles. Periodic elections connote a legislature accountable to the people, as elections are the biggest accountability test for an outgoing government.[34] Free and secret election requirements should be read together in the context of subjective election rights as safeguards from undue interference and manipulation. The rule of law, lawfulness and non-discrimination are the main weapons used by the ECtHR in combating electoral irregularities. Further, pluralistic elections are incumbent on states, as the eighth determinant requires "a choice of the legislature". The article is open-ended in light of the requirement to set up the criteria indispensable for free expression of the will of the people, which represents the final determinant.

Article 3 of Protocol no. 1 imposes a positive obligation on the ratifying states to hold free elections. Simultaneously, it imposes a negative obligation on the states parties to the ECHR to refrain from any conduct which might endanger the free expression of the will of people by, for example, abusing the state funds and resources in an electoral campaign or by keeping political prisoners.[35]

---

[34] Van Dijk, G. J. H. Hoof, Theory and Practice of the European Convention on Human Rights (1998) p. 655.
[35] Harris, Boyle, Warbrick, Law of the European Convention on Human Rights (1995) pp. 19-21.

III. European Regional Organizations Developing Standards in the Election Field

At first glance, Article 3 of the ECHR Protocol no. 1 might appear to contain unqualified rights, its wording not containing legitimate grounds for the interference by the Government. Despite the lack of clear language stipulating any limitations, electoral rights are not absolute.[36] Therefore, the ECtHR considers that the interference with these rights is possible under the margin of appreciation doctrine.

While it imposes several more specific requirements relating to elections, Article 3 of the ECHR Protocol no. 1 is not written in rigid language and does not impose an automatic outcome. Its application is flexible, as confirmed by ECtHR case-law.[37] It follows that ECHR Article 3 of Protocol no. 1 according to its legal form is standard. The evolutive meaning given by the ECtHR to the ECHR relevant article further confirms this argument. There is diversity among the ratifying states regarding their political and legal culture. Therefore, Article 3 of Protocol no. 1 contains the lowest common denominator for conducting "free and fair" elections.

On empirical note, between 1959 and 2009, only 39 violations of Article 3 to Protocol no. 1 were found, out of which the majority of cases (15) were against Italy. This number is considerably lower in comparison to, e.g., the number of violations relating to the right to a fair trial, which have been established in approximately 500 judgments per annum. The low number of violations may be also a consequence of other factors, such as the restrictive scope of the article, delay in proceedings and the active involvement of other international organizations in the election field. However, a surprising increase in the breach of election rights in 2010 and beginning of 2011 has been observed. The ECtHR established nine violations, which constitutes approximately 1/4th of the violations of this article for the period 1959-2009. The increase might be due to an increased accessibility to the ECHR and to increased knowledge about the ECHR protection system in the election arena.[38]

(ii) Case-law and Doctrinal Approach of the ECtHR

---

[36] Jacobs, White, Ovey, The European Convention on Human Rights (4th edition) (2004) pp. 389-390.
[37] See, for example, *Zdanoka v. Latvia.*.
[38] The ECtHR statistics are available at<http://www.coe.int>.

Although the ECtHR is not bound by precedents, the case-law pertaining to Article 3 of Protocol no. 1 to the ECHR is framed by ECtHR judicial doctrine and its interpretative tools. The ECtHR applies a teleological interpretation, in light of the ECHR's objective and spirit, i.e., the protection of human rights and democratic values.[39] Its interpretation is anchored in the "effective political democracy doctrine" set out in the ECHR Preamble. The doctrine's main values are justice, non-violence, peace, freedom, rule of law and effective observance of human rights and fundamental freedoms. It follows that any system promoting and protecting them, in compliance with the requirements set out in Article 3 of the ECHR Protocol no. 1 will be considered compatible with the "effective political democracy doctrine". Inadequate protection of human rights and fundamental freedoms results in diminished democracy.

The ECtHR also applies an evolutive interpretation, meaning that although Article 3, P-1, does not require a particular electoral system, any national electoral system must be assessed in light of the political evolution of the country concerned.[40] Its cases are examined in view of the particular socio-political occurrences in the country and its history in terms of governance with the aim to protect effective and viable democracy and enable free expression of the will of the people.

The ECtHR uses a liberal doctrinal approach regarding the ECHR's procedural requirements. The first argument lies in the acceptance of individual applications under Article 3 of the ECHR Protocol no. 1. The ECtHR has decided that the Protocol affords protection to individuals regarding their subjective electoral rights, as the Convention had to be read as a whole and there had not been a difference in substance between this article and other ECHR articles.[41] The second argument along these lines lies in the wider interpretation of the normative concept of "legislature". It encompasses not only national assemblies, but also regional assemblies with legislative power as well as the EP in view of its role in the supranational decision-making. As a result, this pan-European judicial body effectively protects individual rights in a wider number of cases, relating to the elections of the bodies qualified as a legislature under its case-law.

---

[39] ECtHR, What are the Limits to the Evolutive Interpretation of the Convention? Dialogue between Judges, CoE (2011) pp. 6-7 at <http://www.coe.int>.
[40] Ibid, p. 8.
[41] *Mathieu-Mohin and Clerfayt v. Belgium*.

The ECtHR developed a core judicial doctrine -the margin of appreciation- as its analytical tool.[42] This doctrine indicates what the states decide at local level without the ECtHR interference, as long as they are democratic and have used their power in a reasonable manner.[43] In such a way, the ECtHR pays due attention to the relevant complex historico-political context of each ratifying country. It has repeatedly held that it could not substitute itself for domestic authorities in terms of assessing local needs and conditions, or substitute itself for a legislature, by imposing a legislative measure. It follows that the margin of appreciation reflects the limits that the judges impose on themselves in line with the principle of subsidiarity and the separation of powers doctrine.

The "margin of appreciation doctrine" has also been applied in the adjudication of cases under Article 3 of the ECHR Protocol no. 1. As a rule, the ratifying states enjoy a wide margin of appreciation in the electoral context.[44] It is based on the following three rules:

First, any interference with the qualified rights must be lawful, i.e., rooted in domestic substantive and procedural law, as well as in the ECHR. The law must be of a certain quality (predictable, precise, clear, accessible and adopted in good time before elections). If it gives discretionary powers, their scope and effect must be clearly annunciated.

Second, the interference must pursue a legitimate aim. The ECtHR has accepted a legitimacy of a plurality of aims such as crime prevention, protection of the rule of law, of a language arrangement that was publicly debated, and of national security. In fact, any aim mentioned in other ECHR articles or connected with institutional arrangements that reflect the public good in a democratic society, that is well-reasoned and justified, can be considered legitimate by the ECtHR. Yet, no aim that has a sole goal to punish or humiliate a person can be considered legitimate.[45]

Third, there must be a necessity or pressing social need for the interference. The ECtHR applies the principle of proportionality, as the interference must be proportionate to the

---

[42] Harris, Boyle, Warbrick, Law of the European Convention on Human Rights (1995) p. 12.
[43] Steiner, Alston, International Human Rights in Context, Law, Politics, Morals (2nd edition) (2000) pp. 854-855.
[44] Harris, Boyle, Warbrick, Law of the European Convention on Human Rights (1995) p. 554.
[45] For example, the Italian bankruptcy cases.

legitimate aim sought.[46] The ECtHR conducts a balancing exercise between the right of an individual and protection of the public good. The balancing exercise does not mean that there are no European minimal standards, which the ratifying states must observe. On the contrary, the interference complained of must not be disproportionate or arbitrary to the extent that it thwarts the free expression of the will of the people.[47] The concept of arbitrariness encompasses the abuse of power, unfairness in the procedure and unjustified decisions in the electoral context. It refers to a mismatch between the measure chosen by the authorities and the purpose, even when the motivation for the measure is right.[48]

The case-law presented below[49] further clarifies the elements for proper application of this article.

a. Definition of Legislature

The ECHR only protects election rights for the election of a legislature, i.e., a parliament or regional assembly with legislative powers.[50] The body whose elections are at stake must possess "an inherent primary rulemaking power"[51] to be qualified as legislature. Thus, the ECtHR has come up with the autonomous interpretation of the term "legislature".

In *PY v. France* the elections for the Congress of a French territory were at stake. The ECtHR, similarly to the previous cases, held that the scope of Article 3 of Protocol no. 1 was not limited to the national parliaments. In the instant case, the Congress had the power to initiate legislation, and to adopt status and budget. In conclusion, the ECtHR did not limit the definition of legislature to strictly law-making powers, with the aim of ensuring effective political democracy.

In order to examine whether or not this article should be also applicable for the elections of the EP, the ECtHR examined, whether in view of its powers, the EP should be considered as a legislature. In the case *Matthews v. UK,* the applicant who was from Gibraltar, complained that she was disfranchised from the EP elections, by virtue of the European Community Act.

---

[46] Harris, Boyle, Warbrick, Law of the European Convention on Human Rights (1995) pp. 11-12.
[47] *Mathieu-Mohin and Clerfayt; Gitonas and Others v. Greece;* and *Yumak and Sadak v. Turkey* [GC.]
[48] *Orujov v. Azerbaijan.*
[49] See Annex for the list of ECtHR cases.
[50] *Mathieu-Mohin and Clerfayt v. Belgium;* and *Santoro v. Italy.*
[51] *Booth-Clibborn and others v. UK.*

The ECtHR concluded that the elections for the EP were protected by Article 3 of Protocol no. 1, as the body concerned was a legislature with due regard being given to its principle power of accountability and its decisive role in the creation of the Community legislation. The ECtHR found a violation, as it held that even when a ratifying state transferred competence to an international organization, it still retained the responsibility for protecting rights guaranteed by the ECHR.[52] In spite of the states' enjoyment of a wide margin of appreciation in the choice of electoral systems, the applicant in the instant case was completely denied the opportunity to express her opinion in the elections of the members of EP, although it had a considerable regulatory impact in Gibraltar. The judgment came 5 years after the date of submission of the application, but it had great impact, as it required a change in the UK electoral system, i.e., to allow its citizens to vote for the EP, while ensuring the equality of votes.

The ECtHR declared inadmissible the application of *Ljube Boskovski v. Macedonia* regarding alleged violation of his right to stand for presidential elections, as office of president did not have sufficient powers to qualify as a legislature.

b. The Right to Vote

Although the right to vote can be restricted under the ECHR, no restrictions, such as residence or language requirements, can be used in an arbitrary and discriminatory way, as demonstrated by the cases examined below.

Equality

The case *Mathieu-Mohin and Clerfayt v. Belgium* concerned the elections in the regional councils in Brussels and the requirement to take an oath in the Flemish language, which automatically made the person a member of the Flemish Council. The ECtHR confirmed that the states had a wide margin of appreciation when determining the conditions attached to the election rights. However, the ECtHR had to ascertain whether the election rights were not thwarted to such an extent so as to impair their very essence. No violation was found on the account that the citizens from both communities enjoyed the same conditions for exercise of their election rights, hence the limitations were not disproportionate. The ECtHR took into

---

[52] Jacobs, White, Ovey, The European Convention on Human Rights (4th edition) (2004) p. 30.

consideration the particular institutional arrangements of Belgium, which came as a result of difficult negotiations between the two communities.

Incarcerated Persons

Regardless of the fact that the ECtHR examines election cases from the view point of the political evolution of each country, there are some restrictions of the active election right, which end up in a horizontal prohibition at the European level, with no exceptions.

The ECtHR examined the blanket ban of the prisoners' vote in the cases *Hirst (No. 2) v. the United Kingdom* and *Calmanovici v. Romania*. In both cases the ECtHR found a violation, and considered the impugned blanket ban by law both arbitrary and discriminatory. The individuals were classified as prisoners without the right to vote, but no other relevant circumstances (e.g. the offence for which they were convicted, its seriousness) were being examined. Since such a ban was automatically imposed, there was no assessment of the proportionality, which meant that a person could lose his voting right even in case of a minor violation.

The ECtHR case-law goes hand in hand with the HRC views, which require any deprivation of the voting rights to be temporary. Furthermore, it is more justified to disfranchise persons who tampered with elections or committed a crime when executing public function than in case of a simple traffic accident. As the ECtHR stated, the right to vote is no longer a privilege, but a universal right. The ECtHR re-affirmed these principles in the case of *Frodl v. Austria.*

However, in the cases against Italy it seems, at first glance, that the above more comprehensive approach was abandoned. Namely, in the *Labita* and *Santoro* respectively, the ECtHR scrutinized the restriction on election rights when a person, who was not convicted, was placed under police supervision. The focus was on how the measure was implemented in the particular case, and not its imposition as a general measure. In the *Santoro* case, the ECHR found a violation on account of an unnecessary prolongation of administrative procedure for deleting/reinstating the applicant on the voters' list. In the *Labita* case, the applicant was acquitted of all charges, but he was disfranchised in order to stop voting for the mafia. According to the ECtHR even the fight against the mafia was not a sufficient reason to deprive a person from his voting right when he was cleared of all charges of belonging to the mafia.

Nowhere in the above cases, had the ECtHR stated that exclusion of non-convicts from voting represented, *per se,* a violation of the ECHR, in view of the presumption of innocence protected by it. However, this does not mean that the ECtHR denies either.

Persons with Mental Impairment

In the case *Alajos Kiss v. Hungary*, the applicant who was placed under a guardianship due to his mental state, was disfranchised. The ECtHR took an approach in line with the UNCRPD, which endorses voting rights for persons with mental disability. It found a violation on the account that there was a blanket and automatic prohibition for mentally impaired persons to vote, without any individual examination of their particular circumstances by the authorities.

Residence

The residence requirement was examined in the case *PY v. France,* in the political context of self-determination of a French territory. The election was a part of the package, which ended a difficult security and political situation. The applicant complained about a too lengthy residence requirement to vote for members of the Congress. The ECtHR assessed the length of residence in light of the country's political evolution. It reiterated that the features, which might have been unacceptable for one system might be justified in another due to local conditions under ECHR Article 56 (3), applicable to territories under administration. There was a positive and conclusive proof for the local requirements, which in this case were the history and status of New Caledonia and its process of self-determination.

Although, countries of origin do not have an absolute obligation to give immigrants voting rights, in the case of *Sitaropoulos and Others v. Greece* the respondent state was found in breach of the ECHR. The reason was that no election was organized in the places of residents of the Greek immigrants, despite the Greek Constitution requirement to regulate out-of-country voting. This ECtHR judgment clearly lacks analysis of the available systems of out-of-country voting with, e.g., estimation of the needed resources and funds for their organization, the number of citizens voting abroad at the particular polling stations, the distance they would need to travel to vote, and difficulties in safeguarding free and fair elections in case of postal or electronic voting. Such analysis would help avoid imposing too heavy burden on the state in terms of funds and protection of electoral rights. Unsurprisingly, the judgment was reversed by the Grand Chamber, on account that neither international law nor the Constitution made it mandatory for Greece to allow the voters to vote abroad; the states enjoyed a wide margin of appreciation in this regard; and the applicants were not disproportionally burdened by the impossibility to vote in Greece.

Property

The ECtHR found a violation of election rights against Italy for temporary disenfranchisement of persons who went bankrupt. The Italian cases of *Albanese; Vitello; Bova;* and *Campagnano* refer to this issue. Although bankruptcy proceedings were not of a penal character, the applicants were penalized by being deprived of their constitutional right to vote with the only aim being to humiliate them. It appears that to date, Italy has not taken a general measure to remedy the repetitive violations originating from the suspension of voting rights in case of bankruptcy.

c. The Right to Stand for Elections

States can impose stricter criteria on the passive election right in comparison to those attached to active election right. The ECtHR examined a number of complaints in this regard, ranging from a system of deposits to an election threshold.

Lustration

A number of cases originating in Eastern Europe relate to the ineligibility of the candidates to stand for elections on the basis of their past political activities, or their involvement with the security services of the past regime. The most interesting case concerning lustration is *Zdanoka v. Latvia* where the applicant was declared ineligible to stand for elections due to her former membership in the Communist party which had been banned for an indefinite time. While the case was pending before the ECtHR she won a seat in the EP.

On one hand, the applicant complained that there was nothing in her personal conduct to justify the restriction of her passive election right. On the other hand, the government contended that the restriction pursued a legitimate aim, i.e., protection of democratic order from those who have turned against it and did not respect democratic principles in the past, as well as protection of national security and the state's independence. According to the government, the measure was proportionate, as it only targeted persons who actively participated in the operations threatening Latvia's independence after the attempted coup d'état supported by the applicant's party. The ECtHR Chamber found a violation, as the disqualification from elections was permanent and domestic courts did not have the possibility to examine on individual bases, if the restriction was still proportionate to the aim pursued.

The Grand Chamber reversed the judgment and found that Latvia did not exceed the margin of appreciation. In particular, the authorities were better placed to assess the difficulties when establishing democratic order in view of the country's historico-political context. Moreover, the aim of the ECHR was to protect democratic values and democracy as the only system, so nothing aimed at destruction of these values could attract the protection of the ECHR. As long as the statutory distinction itself was clear, proportionate and not discriminatory regarding the whole category or group specified in the legislation, the task of domestic court could be limited to establishing if the individual belonged to that group. However, in view of the Latvia's current stability, the ECtHR requested the legislature to review the statutory restrictions with aim to bring it to early termination, since in well-established democracies such limitation of the passive election right would be hardly deemed acceptable.

In another case against Latvia, the *Adamsons case,* the applicant occupied posts, which were subordinated to the KGB during the soviet times. After the independence of Latvia, he occupied public posts including MP post. The applicant was declared ineligible to stand for the 2002 elections on the account of his past collaboration with the ex-Soviet Union security bodies. The ECtHR invoked the principles set out in the above Zdanoka case. Therefore, it assessed the relevant legislation depriving the applicant from his right to stand for elections in light of political evolution of the country, i.e., something which was unacceptable in one system, could be justified in the context of another. The ECtHR in light of its previous case-law, recalled the principles for lustration laws, as follows:

First, the lustration law had to be clear, accessible and foreseeable. Second, it should not serve the purpose of punishment, which was the task of the criminal law. Third, the lustration law had to be precise, so that the responsibility is individualized for each person concerned. Finally, the lustration law measures had to be temporary.

In the instant case, the ECtHR established a violation of Article 3 of the ECHR Protocol no. 1, as Latvia overstepped its margin of appreciation. It concluded, *inter alia,* that despite the Grand Chamber's judgment in the *Zdanoka* case indicating that it was sufficient to establish if the applicant belonged to a certain defined group, after a certain period of time such group assessment was not sufficient for the ECHR's purposes. The ECtHR noted that there was no information or evidence that the applicant caused damage to Latvia's independence and its democracy. In addition, the applicant was declared ineligible to be elected 10 years after his military career, during which he had occupied public functions in independent Latvia. The ECtHR also noted that without any explanation the lustration law was extended for additional 10 years, which again affected the applicant.

The facts of the *Zdanoka case* were sufficient for the Grand Chamber to depart from the general principles, which were confirmed also in other cases not relating to lustration. Still, the Grand Chamber requested termination of the measure in view of the ECHR general standards. It does not come as a surprise that in the *Adamsons* case, the ECtHR Chamber followed the reasoning of the *Zdanoka* Chamber judgment, and in some way criticized the Grand Chamber judgment for allowing too wide a margin of appreciation for Latvia, instead of following the established general principles. There is a clear difference between the factual situations in both cases. Whereas in *Zdanoka* the applicant used to be a member of a banned party which had a role to play in the coup d'état and the applicant did not indicate her disagreement with her party's actions, in the latter case the applicant executed a number of important functions in democratic and independent Latvia.

In *Petkov and others v. Bulgaria* the ECtHR limited its examination to the protection of the effectiveness of the legal system and credibility of domestic courts. On the basis of the lustration law exposing ex-collaborators of ex-security agencies, and in accordance with a certificate issued by a competent commission, the applicants were removed from the candidates' list upon their Coalition's requests. In the ensuing proceedings the administrative court quashed the decision of the electoral authorities for removal of the applicants from the candidates' list, as it found that such a decision could have only been based on the Commission's report and not on a certificate. Since the applicants were not reinstated on the candidates' lists, they complained that the refusal of the authorities to comply with the administrative court's final judgment infringed their passive election right under article 3 of

Protocol no. 1. The ECtHR affirmed that any limitations imposed with respect to passive election rights had to be consistent with the rule of law and surrounded by sufficient safeguards against arbitrariness and abuse of power. It established a breach of Article 3 of the ECHR Protocol no. 1 on the account that conduct of the authorities undermined the effectiveness of the legal system. This ECtHR judgment aimed at preserving the authority of the courts as a branch of government in view of the separation of powers doctrine.

Illegal Activities

In Etxebarria Barrena Arza Nafarroako Autodeterminazio Bilgunea and Aiarako and Others v. Spain and other 2009 similar judgments against Spain, the election candidates' nomination was annulled by domestic court, as the main aim of their political activity was to pursue the purposes of illegal parties. The legitimate aim for the interference was to protect democracy, and the measure used was proportional to the aim pursued, since the assessments were made individually and the measures were imposed according to the individual situation. As a result, some of the complaints were accepted by domestic courts on the basis that no sufficiently strong link was established as existing between the candidates and the dissolved parties. For those whose complaints were rejected, on the basis of evidence domestic courts established that they intended to pursue activities of dissolved parties that were supporting violence and activities of ETA. Furthermore, in regional governments there were representatives advocating political independence, which meant that there was no intention by the Spanish Government to prohibit all manifestations of the idea of independence.

The ECtHR in this case also adhered to its general principles of individualization, non-violence and protection of the freedom of expression.

The former Commission of Human Rights examined whether or not the decision to withdraw individual's election rights on account of his or her previous activities constituted a violation of Article 3 of Protocol No. 1. For example, it declared inadmissible the applications *X. v. the Netherlands, X. v. Belgium* and *Van Wambeke v. Belgium*[53], where the applicants, who had been convicted following the Second World War of collaboration with the enemy or treason, were permanently deprived of election rights. The Commission considered that the purpose

---

[53] Application no. 6573/74, Commission decision of 19 December 1974, DR 1, p. 88; Application no. 8701/79, Commission decision of 3 December 1979, DR 18, p. 250 and Application no. 16692/90, Commission decision of 12 April 1991.

of legislation depriving persons convicted of treason of certain political rights was to ensure that persons who had seriously abused in wartime their right to participate in public life, were prevented in future from abusing their political rights in a manner prejudicial to the security of the state or the foundations of a democratic society. Similarly, in the case of *Glimmerveen and Hagenbeek v. the Netherlands,* the Commission declared inadmissible the applications concerning the refusal to allow the applicants, who were the leaders of a proscribed organisation with racist and xenophobic affiliation, to stand for election, as the applicants "intended to participate in these elections and to avail themselves of the right for a purpose which the Commission [had] found to be unacceptable".

From the above cases, it is clear that the ECtHR attaches the greatest importance to the legal gurantees for election rights and plurality of choice for the voters. Yet, the red line of participation in and connection with the activities inciting violance and religious and racial haterd must not be crossed. When there is a criminal conviction for serious criminal cases, deprivation of election rights could be one of the measures imposed for a legitimate aim, e.g., preservation of security and democratic order, or the rights of others. As a rule, no one should be permanently deprived of election rights.

The cases of *Abil v. Azerbaijan* and *Atakishi v. Azerbaijan* examined the question of disqualification of an electoral candidate against whom there were allegations of bribe and of stirring-up social, racial, ethnic or religious hatred and hostility by his electoral campaign. The ECtHR reiterated its previous case-law where in order to disqualify a candidate, the authorities had to offer sufficient safeguards against arbitrariness and provide good reasons in line with the rule of law principle. The ECtHR found a number of procedural errors, as well as a wrongful characterization of the alleged offence for which the applicant was disqualified from the election. One of the reasons the ECtHR found violations in both cases was the lack of sufficient and relevant evidence to disqualify a candidate. Whereas under Article 6 of the ECHR, the ECtHR does not assess the evidence and does not act as a fourth instance court, when the passive electoral right is at stake, the ECtHR scrutinizes in-depth the proofs of the alleged electoral fraud in line with the principles laid down in the case of the *Orujov v. Azerbaijan* judgment. These principles say that when electoral candidates are disqualified because of a suspicion of illegal activities, the authorities must display due diligence regarding the standard of proof against the electoral candidate and the relevant legal remedies must be adequate, impartial and effective. Otherwise, electoral candidates might be easily disqualified from the election by unfounded allegations of fraud.

Although a violation of the ECHR relevant article was found in the above-mentioned cases, the judgments came 6 to 7 years after the elections, and thus did not represent an adequate redress for the applicants.

In the case of *Paksas v. Lithuania,* the applicant was barred from running in elections, as he had been impeached by the Constitutional Court, during his presidency. The ECtHR did not accept the argument of the Government that in the election cases a wide margin of appreciation ought to be granted to the states without a long democratic tradition. According to the ECtHR, such a strict impeachment rule represented an exception in Europe.

Dual Citizenship

The case of *Tănase and Chirtoacă v. Moldova,* concerned the inability of persons with multiple nationalities to stand as candidates in parliamentary elections or to take the office, by virtue of legislation. The ECtHR agreed that the legitimate aim for the measure was to ensure the loyalty to the State, but not to the government as the latter must be held accountable by the MPs. The amendments to the law introduced less than a year before elections was especially detrimental to the opposition. Moldova was the only country, which allowed dual nationality and yet prohibited those persons from being MPs. The ECtHR established a violation, *inter alia*, as for ensuring loyalty Moldova could use less strict measures not affecting the free expression of the people's will.

In an earlier case against the UK concerning the right to stand for elections for citizens with dual citizenship, no breach of the ECHR was found, as it only concerned a restriction for persons who had already been a member of the legislature in another country.

Electoral Deposits

The ECtHR examined the question of electoral deposits in the case of *Sukhovetskyy v. Ukraine* and found no violation. It held that deposits pursued a legitimate aim, i.e., an effective, streamlined, serious representation, whilst avoiding the unreasonable outlay of public funds. In addition, there was a serious public debate before this measure was adopted, and it was subject of considerable parliamentary and constitutional court's scrutiny. The ECtHR considered that in the particular circumstances the deposits were not an obstacle to pluralism, or an impenetrable administrative or financial barrier.

Conflict of Interest

In *Ahmed and others v. UK* the authorities introduced a regulation restricting political activities for certain higher categories of local civil servants. They were, *inter alia,* prohibited from standing for local, national and European elections and from campaigning. The ECtHR did not find a violation of Article 3 of Protocol no. 1, considering that election rights were not absolute and the states imposed different criteria for their enjoyment. The restriction complained of was not found to be disproportionate, as it pursued a legitimate aim, i.e., to avoid any appearance of bias with respect to execution of duties by local civil servants, and it was of a temporary character. As a result, it did not impair the free expression of the opinion of the people. It seems that although the UK law could have foreseen the absence of leave for the affected civil servants until the election results were known, it does not appear that the lack of such a rule upset the balance between the choice of the electorate and the requirement for impartiality and loyalty of civil servants. Even more so, such an opportunity still provides an open door for abuse of the position by misuse of public funds, nepotism and providing partisan advice due to the loyalty owed to the party, which in some instances might be difficult to control.

Azerbaijani law does not allow clergyman while engaged in professional religious activities to run in various types of elections. In the case of *Seyidzade v. Azerbaijan* although the applicant resigned from his post, his nomination as electoral candidate was rejected based on the above law. The ECtHR based its judgment on the lack of quality of the law, which it found lacking foreseeability in the electoral context.

The case *Kovach v. Ukraine* concerned the invalidation of votes obtained by the leading candidate in several electoral districts, which resulted in his losing the election. The ECtHR established a violation holding that the invalidation was arbitrary. The main reason for its decision was the lack of clarity of the respective legislation, which empowered the electoral commissions to invalidate votes on the basis of "other circumstances which made it impossible to establish the wishes of the voters".

Untrue Information Supplied by the Candidate

A number of cases with various factual situations were examined under Article 3 of Protocol no. 1 concerning a refusal to confirm a candidate for elections based on untrue information submitted by him or her. For example, in the case of _Russian Conservative Party of Entrepreneurs and Others v. Russia,_ the applicant party candidates' list was refused since some of the leading candidates submitted untrue information about their property. Despite the fact that the ensuing judicial proceedings were favorable to the applicant party, upon a prosecutor's supervisory request the judicial decisions were reversed to the applicant's detriment. The ECtHR found a violation on two accounts: 1) that extraordinary supervision requested by the prosecutor was against the principle of legal certainty when there was a final judgment in the case, and 2) that the applicant party and the second applicant, although had not breached the election law, had to bear consequences which were disproportionate to the legitimate aim sought, i.e., true information from the candidates about their financial situation. However, the ECtHR rejected the complaint alleging violation of the right to vote for the party applicant, holding, _inter alia,_ that the plurality of the choice was preserved in the elections.

It appears that the ECtHR did not answer the substance of the complaint, i.e., that due to the unlawful interference of the authorities with the guarantees of Article 3 to Protocol no. 1 as ascertained by the ECtHR, the applicant was unable to cast his vote for the initial option of his own choosing. In order to ascertain whether or not the plurality of choice was indeed preserved, the ECtHR had to embark on the analysis of political programmes, options and relations between the parties in the country, for which it was not equipped and which would have made it enter the field of political analysis.

In _Melnychenko against Ukraine_, another case in connection with furnishing untrue information, the ECtHR again established a breach of the ECHR. The case concerned an applicant against whom criminal proceedings were started for the alleged disclosure of confidential information to the opposition, and who was granted asylum in another state. At the next legislative elections the opposition nominated him. Because he was not in Ukraine, his candidature was rejected although he had a permanent residence there. The ECtHR considered that the electoral body should not have blindly followed the law requiring a 5-year residence in the country, but should have taken into consideration the special situation in which the applicant found himself, i.e., that he had to leave the country, fearful of political persecution.

In the *Krasnov and Skuratov v. Russia* the ECtHR agreed with the Government that the measure was proportionate to the aim pursued with respect to the first applicant, since he knowingly submitted untrue information that could have affected voters' ability to make an informed choice. The aim to have true information about the election candidates and to avoid any misrepresentations to the voters seems sufficient to reject the complaint. Regarding the second applicant, the ECtHR found a breach of the ECHR on the account that the decisions rejecting the candidacy failed to meet the Convention standards of lawfulness and foreseeability. Unlike the above Russian case regarding the first applicant, in the *Sarykhanuan v. Armenia* the ECtHR noted that there was no ill-will or intention from the candidate to conceal the information, which was minor for the candidacy. A violation of Article 3 of Protocol no. 1 was found since no reasoned assessment, corroborated with evidence was made by the domestic courts regarding the particular circumstances of the applicant.

Electoral Fraud

In the *Georgian Labour Party v. Georgia,* a political party complained about a compilation of the voters' lists, the composition of electoral commissions and the annulment of elections in two constituencies, without their repetition. Despite concluding that there was a fundamental flaw regarding the manner of the establishment of the election administration, and despite, *mutatis mutandis,* requirement for objective institutional independence under Article 6, the ECtHR still required concrete evidence of abuse by the election administration. The ECtHR found a violation of the applicant party's right to stand for election on the ground of the annulment of the parliamentary elections in two constituencies and the failure to repeat them. Such conduct effectively deprived a large number of voters from casting their ballot, while at the same time impairing the expression of the free will of the voters. The ECtHR held that regardless of security problems, the state concerned still had an obligation to conduct free and fair elections country-wide. This was true even more so, since it did not declare a derogation under ECHR's Article 15.

In the case of *Namat Aliyev v. Azerbaijan* the applicant complained about a number of irregularities on the election day, which made it impossible to determine the true opinion of the voters and infringed his passive election right. The ECtHR rejected the Government's argument that even if there were election irregularities they would have not effected the election outcome, as it found that what was at stake was not who would win the election, but the individual's right to stand for office. The ECtHR found a violation because the electoral commission left the applicant's complaint unexamined, and the appeals and supreme courts instead of investigating his subsequent appeals, rejected them for purely formalistic reasons. Similarly, in another *Azerbaijani* case[54] a violation was found when authorities did not process the irregularities in a fair and impartial manner, which resulted in the annulment of elections to the detriment of the winning candidate who in no way participated in the commission of those irregularities. In fact, it transpires from the circumstances of this case, that the irregularities were committed with the purpose to deprive the winning opposition candidate of his right to occupy an office. So, it was not only the individual's right to stand for elections what was at stake, but also the voters' choice about who was fit and trustworthy to occupy elected public office.

Mandate Entrusted to the Wining Candidate

A surprisingly large number of ECHR cases deal with the termination of a mandate of regularly elected officials. For example, in *Lykourezos v. Greece* the applicant, a practicing lawyer, was elected an MP. However, after entry into force of the legislation that proscribed professional activity with the aim of avoiding conflicts of interest for MPs, his mandate was terminated. The ECtHR found a violation on the grounds that Article 3 of Protocol no. 1 guaranteed also the individual's right to occupy the office, once elected, and that the later disqualification was not foreseeable.

Again, the ECtHR based its reasoning on the rule of law argument, by stating that no subsequent amendments to the organization of electoral system could call the choice of the voters into question, except for compelling democratic reasons, which did not exist in the

---

[54] *Kerimova v. Azerbaijan; Mammadov v. Azerbaijan* (no. 2) and *Hajili v. Azerbaijan.*

instant case. The applicant was awarded damages, but it is unclear if he was re-instated as an MP, in line with the ECtHR's judgment.

In *the Paschalidis, Koutmeridis and Zaharakis v. Greece* the ECtHR again found a breach of the right of elected MPs to occupy the office. The Greek court changed its previous decision regarding the rules of tabulation and decided that blank ballots had to be counted. As a consequence, the seats already won by the applicants were re-allocated and they lost their mandates. However, in other parts of Greece the blank ballots were not counted, which put the MPs in an unequal position. As shown in the above cases, the ECtHR often bases its reasoning on the foreseeability requirement of the legislation, as one of the rule of law elements.

In yet another case against Greece, *Gitonas* and others, elected public officials could not occupy their posts, because of the rules not allowing public functions to be cumulated for a certain period of time. The applicants had managerial posts with public media, social security office and posts under supervision of the Prime Minister. A special court annulled their election to avoid conflict of interest. The aim was to ensure freedom from abusive advantages to the detriment of others and to protect others from undue pressures coming from persons in decision-making positions. The ECtHR found that the Greek court had reasonable motives when it decided to annul the elections. Further, the annulment was not contrary to the Greek legislation, as it was neither arbitrary nor disproportionate and did not thwart the free expression of the people. Therefore, no violation was found. In view of other ECtHR cases which were decided later and according to which higher protection should be afforded to already-elected candidates, one question immediately comes up, although it was not addressed by the ECtHR. Why did the Greek authorities not react earlier, at the stage when the applicants were not yet confirmed as election candidates, if the conflict of interest was so clear from the outset?

In the case of *Ilicak v. Turkey* the ECtHR found a violation when the applicant's mandate was terminated, because she belonged to a political party, which was dissolved. However, she and the applicant in the case of *Kavakci v. Turkey* complained that the real reason why their mandates were terminated was their wearing a veil in the parliament. Although the ECtHR agreed that protection of laicism, as well as protection of the rights of others was a legitimate aim, it established a violation, *inter alia*, on the account that the loss of a mandate was a very strict penalty. According to the ECtHR, the authorities had to react before the candidates were confirmed.

Drawing a parallel between these cases and the previous Spanish cases, it is clear that the ECtHR attaches higher guarantees to Article 3 of the ECHR Protocol no. 1 in cases when the applicants are already elected. Still, in view of the fact that the ECtHR interprets the ECHR based on all its provisions, the analysis of the situation of the women's rights in Turkey from the viewpoint of protection of the rights of others and the right to worship seems to be missing in the reasoning of the above judgments against Turkey. Perhaps it is better to have a woman-MP with a veil, than not to have any female MPs at all.

In *Gaulidier v. Slovakia* the applicant was made to sign a resignation letter with no date, before his election as MP. When he left his party, the letter was sent to the parliament that accepted his resignation, in spite of the applicant's denial. Although the constitutional court decided that the applicant could not be deprived of his seat under these circumstances because of the lack of genuine will to resign, it lacked the jurisdiction to quash the impugned parliamentary resolution. The case ended with a friendly settlement, a monetary compensation and a press release by the government and the Prime Minister regretting that the applicant could not obtain a redress in the situation.

In the *Selim Sadak and Others v. Turkey* the ECtHR examined the situation when the dissolution of a political party meant forfeiting the parliamentary seats of the applicants, who were militating for Kurdish rights. In accordance with its consistent approach regarding similar cases, the ECtHR found a violation holding, *inter alia,* that the loss of mandate was a disproportionate sever penalty and that domestic courts failed to examine personal political activities of each applicant. In addition, the measure used by the Turkish authorities infringed the rights of the electorate who elected the applicants.

Representation of Minorities

In the case *Aziz against Cyprus* which also concerned a right to vote of a member of a minority, the ECtHR found a violation. The latter case differed in the sense that there was no possibility whatsoever for the Turkish Cypriots to vote in parliamentary elections, while in the Belgian case there was a mechanism in place allowing French-speaking persons to exercise their election rights. Despite the fact that the division on two voters' lists based on ethnicity was an institutional arrangement like in the Belgian case, the ECtHR found that while the factual situation changed, the legislation remained the same, thus excluding the applicant from the voters' list solely on the basis of his ethnicity. The ECtHR requested Cyprus to implement an inevitable election reform, in addition to the damages awarded. Indeed, Cyprus adopted new electoral legislation giving equal voting rights to its citizens of Turkish origin.[55]

In *Yumak and Sadak v. Turkey,* the ECtHR examined if the electoral threshold of 10% applied nationwide in the parliamentary elections was too high. Like in the previous cases the ECtHR, including Grand Chamber, relied heavily on the aim, i.e., to strengthen the government stability in light of the specific political context and the foreseeability of the law in question. The *amicus curiae* confirmed that such a high threshold made it impossible for the Kurdish parties to obtain any seats in the national parliament, and was contrary to the ECHR requirement that various political parties be ensured a reasonable opportunity to present their candidates at national elections. The ECtHR found that the constitutional court was providing a safeguard and a balance by seeking the point of equilibrium between the principle of fair representation and governmental stability. Even the fact that Turkey had the highest threshold in Europe, not consistent with election standards, and which effectively deprived a minority from being represented in the Parliament which adopted the laws affecting them, was not sufficient to persuade the ECtHR that Turkey overstepped the margin of appreciation.

In this context, it should be born in mind that the ECHR was not conceived as an instrument for the protection of collective minority rights, but for the protection of individuals. The ECtHR examines the cases through the prism of individual rights. Therefore, other international mechanisms must be activated for the protection of collective minority rights. Still in *Grosaru v. Romania,* the ECtHR examined the rights of the Italian minority to elect its representative via the applicant, a member of that minority. However, the application was

---

[55] Ministers' Deputies Decisions, CM/Del/Dec(2007)997 20 June 2007, Resolution CM/ResDH(2007)77.

examined from the angle of the rule of law requirement, i.e., how precise and clear the applicable law was, and a violation was found on that account.

In *Podkolzina v. Latvia,* the ECtHR determined that this article protected individual, and not collective rights, despite the language requirements. It considered that the restriction pursued a legitimate aim, i.e., effective work in the legislature for which sufficient knowledge of the official language was indispensable. A violation was established on the ground that the decision to deprive the applicant of a passive election right was not proportionate to the aim pursed. The body that certified the knowledge of the language was not impartial, it took arbitrary decisions, and thus abused its power.

Lastly, in *Sejdik and Finci v. Bosnia and Herzegovina* the Grand Chamber examined the rejection of two electoral candidates not belonging to the "nationality of the constitutive people of the country" as required by the Constitution. A violation was found on the basis that the rejection complained of was not proportionate to the aim pursued i.e., return of peace in the country. Evenmore so, that the applicants were discriminated in the performance of their passive election right.

In conclusion, the ECHR offers limited protection of the right to participate in public affairs in terms of the type of elections. The length of proceedings before the ECtHR and the type of remedy that can be awarded give the impression that the ECHR is not necessarily the most adequate and effective instrument in the context of elections. It also appears that due to the wide margin of appreciation given to the states, sometimes it is difficult to discern from the ECtHR case-law wider standards in this field, which are common to the CoE region. Nevertheless, over the years the ECtHR has continuously and increasingly scrutinized the states' margin of appreciation.[56]

At any rate, the ECtHR effectively executes the most important competence vested with them, i.e., judicial protection of the first dimension (election rights) Europe-wide. The ECtHR case-law provides a guidance to authorities on how to regulate elections and apply the law in order to conduct elections in compliance with the European standards.

---

[56] Jacobs, White, Ovey, The European Convention on Human Rights (4th edition) (2004) p. 399.

III. European Regional Organizations Developing Standards in the Election Field

From the cases relating to the voting rights of mentally disabled persons, prisoners and lustrated persons, red lines regarding election cases can be discerned. It is clear that any permanent, non-individualized or discriminatory ban of the enjoyment of electoral rights does not fall within the ambit of the acceptable margin of appreciation.

Another red line is formulated in the Spanish cases cited-above. The ECtHR will never accept any use of violence that will result in abuse and even destruction of the human rights guaranteed by the ECHR, in line with the "Militant Democracy Doctrine".[57]

Protection of minorities, which as a rule is connected with national security and safety, follows the general line formulated in the ECHR. From the Turkish cases cited-above, it follows that the protection of minorities goes hand in hand with state laity, intimately connected with a democratic form of government. On one hand, "democratic laity" allows for an effective enjoyment of religious rights, and on the other hand it enables effective governance of state affairs by avoiding heavy fragmentation in the multicultural societies. Although minority rights as a rule belong to collective rights, the ECtHR has pronounced on them from the angle of individual rights. The efforts to widen the scope of the ECHR by adding a new Protocol on minority rights has remained fruitless. For precisely that reason, the ECtHR should take a more liberal substantive approach and increase its scrutiny of the margin of appreciation in order to protect effectively the rights of minority groups. However, in the cases involving minorities, which are connected with a social conflict and may threaten national security and affect the rights of others, the ECtHR has taken a cautious approach.

Further discussion relating to the maneuvering space of the states includes the case-law relating to the submission of untrue information by the candidates. The ECtHR held that the disqualification of candidates, who submitted such information with no ill – intention or just happened to be on the candidates' list that was annulled due to untrue information, was a disproportionate measure. On the basis of the above ECtHR case-law, deleting the disclosure requirement for the fear of candidates being disqualified, would be a disproportionate measure in and on itself, as it runs contrary to the informed voters' requirement. The public

---

[57] Harvey, Militant Democracy and the European Convention on Human Rights, European Law Review (2004) 29(3) pp. 407-420.

must know which of the candidates it can trust and who deserves to be entrusted with a mandate.

The ECtHR's cautious approach towards the protection of political rights in comparison to the protection of civil rights has resulted in allowing a wider margin of appreciation to the ratifying states in the electoral context. Nonetheless, in some instances, the margin of appreciation doctrine does not appear to be theoretically coherent and intrinsically sound such as in the cases like *Yumak and Sadak v. Turkey* or *Zdanoka v. Latvia.* Still, detours like these ones are well reasoned and justified in line with the principles of greater clarity and consistency in the application of the European rules of the electoral game.

A word of caution, a differentiating treatment may lead to a result where no unified election standards on European soil seem possible. To avoid this jeopardy, the ECtHR should declare a breach of the ECHR whenever the minimal election standards in a particular case are lowered, even as a temporary exception. It can suspend the imposition of a penalty for a reasonably acceptable period of time, until the particular conditions warranting such an exception have expired. This change in approach would be a good defense against the double standards' arguments, i.e., that stricter standards are applied when developed democracies are sued in comparison to developing democracies. Simultaneously, the ECtHR should not be discouraged by the problems it encounters with the implementation of its judgments, which have the effect of diminishing its protection in the arena of electoral rights.[58]

Indeed, the ECtHR did not allow Bosnia and Herzegovina to "get a free ride" and to be excused from the ECHR standards because of its particular political arrangement. The ECtHR found the electoral system discriminatory for any citizen who was not a Bosniak, a Serb or a Croat, as it barred smaller communities from standing in presidential and legislative elections.

(iii) Deduced European Standards in Election Field

---

[58] *Greens and M.T. v. the United Kingdom.*

III. European Regional Organizations Developing Standards in the Election Field

The ECHR's normative content and its reflection in case-law, represent pillars of the European standards in the election field, as underscored in the European electoral heritage. Its election standards are comprehensive and relate to all phases of the electoral cycle: pre-election phase, election day and post-election phase, as follows:

Pre-election Phase

Electoral law and system: The ECHR requires effective political democracy as a political system. Article 3 of Protocol no. 1 dictates the manner for installing such a system of governance, through direct election of the representatives of one chamber of a legislature.

The ECHR does not require a specific electoral system. Electoral thresholds are not considered incompatible by the ECtHR. Their compatibility with the ECHR is assessed in accordance with the reality on the ground, and the need for a stronger and more coherent government. There is an inherent tension between the need to prevent the government from fragmentation and the free expression of the will of the electorate. The attempts to balance this tension have resulted in a variety of electoral systems, considered the best suited in light of the particularities of a country, by the political elites. All these systems are acceptable under Article 3 of P-1, as long as they fulfill its overall standard of "free and fair" elections and satisfy the principle of non-discrimination.

Article 3 of Protocol no. 1 to the ECHR does not foresee special arrangements for ethnic or religious minorities, or women. From the ECtHR case-law[59] the only clear standard that can be discerned in this respect refers to the equal treatment of members of minorities with the rest of the population. Any unfair treatment is prohibited. Any exception in the treatment must be objective and reasonably justified in the given politico-sociological context. Equality of treatment and the non-discrimination principles must be also respected.

The standard referred to by the ECtHR is "a fair representation"[60] which is less stringent requirement than "a meaningful representation". Should the latter have been the standard accepted under the ECHR, it would have required closer scrutiny of the margin of

---

[59] *Mathieu-Mohin and Clerfayt v. Belgium*; the *Etxebarria Barrena Arza Nafarroako Autodeterminazio Bilgunea and Aiarako and Others v. Spain;* and *Sejdik and Finci v. Bosnia and Herzegovina.*
[60] *Yumak and Sadak v. Turkey.*

51

appreciation. It would have required electoral arrangements allowing for a wider representation of minorities, women and ideological groups, as well as greater influence on the Government. Such a standard would have required an ECHR amendment; and presently there is no political will to increase the relevant standards by way of a legally-binding instrument. Nonetheless, human rights' inclusive trend of minorities and women in public decision-making deserves to be reflected normatively in the European key human rights instrument. The hypothetical abuse of rights by groups enjoying the right to meaningful representation cannot be regarded as a valid argument against increasing election standards. Other ECHR protection mechanisms will counter-balance any attempts to destroy what has already been granted in terms of rights.

The stability of electoral law[61] in its key components does not mean that the law should remain unchanged, but rather that legislative changes should be made preferably a year before elections. The electoral law should be also drafted and adopted in light of the requirement for the expression of free will of the people. It is indispensable that various interests be taken into consideration when drafting the law. The ECtHR has repeatedly requested that electoral laws be accessible, precise and foreseeable. Changes in electoral law must not result in a termination of the mandate of a freely elected candidate, as it impairs the essence of election rights.

The court-made law does not impose a requirement for the countries to organize out-of-country voting, when no such provisions have been made in domestic law.[62] On the contrary, if there is a clear legislative requirement the national institutions cannot escape its implementation.

Voters: The subjective right to vote is a universal one. It is not an unqualified right, but it might be subject to reasonable requirements (such as age or nationality) and individualized assessments (with respect to mental capacity[63]). The non-discrimination obligation also applies.

---

[61] *Lykourezos v. Greece*.
[62] *Sitaropoulos and Others v. Greece.*
[63] *Alajos Kiss v. Hungary.*

III. European Regional Organizations Developing Standards in the Election Field

Article 3 of the ECHR Protocol no. 1 contains wording about the criteria enabling a free expression of the will of the people. In this wording, several implicit standards are read, as follows: voters must be secure, free from pressure, manipulation, threats or violence.

When the above wording is read in conjunction with the universality requirements, it fleshes out the standards connected with the voters' list. It must not be an obstacle to casting the vote, but must accurately and lawfully register all and only eligible voters. There will be no obstacles to the ECtHR examining in substance hypothetical voter's allegations about being threatened or effectively disfranchised due to voters' list inaccuracy.

However, a hypothetical individual complaint that a voter was not well-informed about the political programs or about the voting procedure will be hardly admissible, unless other circumstances demonstrate that it concerns a systematic violation, impairing the essence of an active election right. Nonetheless, a well-educated and informed voter is implied by Article 3 of Protocol no. 1.

Candidates: The plurality of electoral options and the universality of the passive election right requires lively political competition. The passive election right is not an absolute one, but is subject to reasonable restrictions (such as age or additional conditions for performance of public office).

The restrictions that do not represent an impenetrable obstacle for the parties and oppositionists, or unfairly exclude them, will be considered compatible with the ECHR. Such restrictions include electoral deposits, disclosure of personal information about the candidates, accumulation of public offices, or holding positions that can enable the candidate to have unfair advantage over other candidates. The restrictions pursue reasonable policies of transparency, of equal treatment of all electoral competitors and of viable electoral competition.

Even collaboration with a non-democratic regime or membership in a dissolved political party cannot disqualify a candidate automatically and indefinitely. Any such additional requirement to execute public office must be clearly stipulated in law and accordingly implemented. In this context, the ECtHR also examines if the state provides sufficient space for a political debate regarding pressing social problems. As a bottom line, the ECHR protection cannot be afforded to applicants who seek to destroy the very rights enunciated therein under a pre-text that their rights were breached.

Electoral Administration: The independence and impartiality of electoral administration is a condition, *sine qua non,* for holding free and fair elections. However, the ECtHR applies a different test from the one under ECHR Article 6 that is valid for the courts. If there is no separation of powers in the institutional set-up, a violation of Article 6 is established. The Code of Good Practice in Electoral Matters, on which the ECtHR relies in the interpretation of the election standards, requires an unbiased and independent electoral administration. Yet, the ECtHR goes further requiring actual proof of abuse of power by the electoral administration, even when its set up does not fulfill the standards for "impartial and independent" body. The ECtHR seems to have made a choice not to assess *in abstracto* the independence and impartiality of the electoral administration bodies, in view of the variety of the models in the CoE countries.[64]

Electoral Campaign: When reading Article 3 of the ECHR Protocol no. 1 in light of its object and as an integral part of the ECHR, it follows that no free expression of the voters is possible without free media and media access under equal conditions for the candidates. Indeed, no breach was found when a winning candidate who held a managerial post with the public media was disqualified because of a conflict of interest.

Effective Legal Protection: The ECtHR has reiterated the importance of effective legal protection. It is not enough to have legal remedies and judicial review for the protection of election rights which are only formally in place. The bodies tasked with legal protection must be independent and impartial and refrain from any abuse.[65] The ECtHR re-affirms that there is no true democracy without adherence to the rule of law doctrine.

Election Day

---

[64] *Namat Aliyev v. Azerbaijan.*
[65] *Georgian Labour Party v. Georgia.*

Voters: Voters' secrecy and security is a continuing requirement on Election Day, as is the voters' right to have an equal opportunity to cast their vote. These principles, not only commit the election administration to act lawfully and responsibly, but also require the same from the police, the media and the political parties.

Regarding distinct groups of voters like prisoner, the ECtHR came up with clear standards. Any indefinite automatic ban on prisoners' voting is considered incompatible with the ECHR. Any temporary ban on their election rights must be proportional to the offence. It must be imposed only in correlation with a conviction for a serious crime, or an election-related offense. While the ECtHR's jurisprudence does not give a simple yes or no answer when a detainee's election rights are at stake, it does make clear that when there is no criminal conviction, no electoral exclusion is justifiable.

Regarding the mentally impaired persons, the standard says that they must be enfranchised to the extent possible based on the individual assessment of their health condition.

Post-election phase

Effective Resolution of Electoral Disputes: A proceeding must fulfill the standard of fairness, hence no undue burden should be placed on individuals in the electoral context. Electoral remedy, which has the effect of invalidating elections that do reflect the will of people, shall not be considered adequate and effective, but merely a tool in the hands of persons wanting to falsify elections. A judicial remedy must not only be available for the resolution of electoral disputes, but must also be adequate and effective.[66]

The mandate entrusted to a winning candidate: The mandate must be given to the candidate who won the elections in line with the electoral system formula. Therefore, any post-electoral violence must be effectively suppressed by the state.

Once a mandate is entrusted to a winning candidate in elections, the maneuvering space of countries becomes restricted. If the mandate of a winner in elections is terminated because of, e.g., a retroactive application of a law or unprecedented court interpretation, the right to run in elections will only be illusory and not effective.

---

[66] *Kerimova v. Azerbaijan*; *Mammadov v. Azerbaijan* (no. 2).

III. European Regional Organizations Developing Standards in the Election Field

The discussion now opens up to the positive and negative sides of the European standards in the elections field, deduced from the ECHR and ECtHR case-law. The positive side first lies in the form of the act in which the standards are set out, which makes it a key source of legally-binding election standards. The unique robust enforcement mechanism is the second limb for an effective protection of subjective election rights.

Second, Article 3 of the ECHR Protocol no. 1 in conjunction with other ECHR rights and freedoms, provides a sufficient legal framework to conduct free and fair elections. There exists a common election denominator, absent of which a regime cannot be called democratic.

Third, the application of the electoral standard of "free and fair" responsive to the countries' local politico-social realities is an added value, provided that the ECtHR maintains its case-by-case impartial and well-justified approach. The ECtHR is not blind to the fact that various European sub-regions share different realities. Moreover, electoral law and practice vary from one country to another depending on the history, tradition, political elites and system of governance. A rigid top-down approach without adequate support in the field would not help countries fulfill the "free and fair" election standard.

On a negative side, not all countries in Europe are bound by the above-mentioned standards. Some of the countries that are OSCE participating states are not CoE members. Furthermore, not all CoE members have ratified the Protocol no. 1 of the ECHR. In such cases, the ECHR remains a standard-setting instrument, strengthening the value of the election standards prescribed in UN or OSCE documents.

The ECHR gives a sufficient legal framework for free and fair elections, provided that there is political will. However, a perfect legal framework is insufficient, and the real challenge lies in its proper implementation. Bearing this in mind, Article 3 of Protocol no. 1 has its constraints. In particular, the standards for electoral law, non-discrimination, universality of voting rights, secrecy, periodicity, judicial protection, resolution of disputes and taking up electoral office are much better developed in comparison to the standards relating to the media, representation of minorities and women, electoral campaign and financing. The latter electoral elements remain a grey area. For example, a fair electoral financing is a key to "free and fair elections". Although it has implicitly done so, the ECtHR has not yet had a chance to explicitly deal with this issue. In light of Article 10 on freedom of expression, the ECtHR might hypothetically disapprove of any ceiling on electoral campaign funding and expenses in line with the US doctrine on freedom of expression applicable to electoral matters,[67] or may follow the GRECO desiderata to limit the electoral campaign spending and incomes in order effectively to prevent and combat corruption in politics.[68]

Elections are like a magic hat. Although they look simple on the surface, the more one digs in, the more rules are required in order to satisfy the "free and fair" election standard. As a consequence, electoral fraud might occur due to the lack of elaborated election standards, if the ECtHR remained the only protection at the level of Europe.

Another lacuna in the ECHR is the lack of a meaningful representation standard. Whereas the ECtHR speaks about fair representation in its case-law, the ECHR Preamble speaks about effective political democracy. Yet, it appears that it is too early to include the standard of a meaningful representation in a legally-binding-treaty, although its composite elements have been subject of a prolonged international debate. Nonetheless, meaningful representation is an aspiring element of the definition of "effective political democracy".

Along the same lines, it is perplexing that despite the Preamble, the right to "free and fair elections" was not originally a part of the ECHR, but it was only later added in a Protocol. Furthermore, no other elements of the right to participate in public affairs, such as the right to direct participation in the decision-making, or the right to access to civil service are found in the ECHR, although they are pillars of the effective political democracy.

The bottom line is that the intention of the ECHR drafters was not to draft an international instrument that would contain detailed standards for all the phases of the electoral cycle. In such a case, it would have been an election standards Convention. On the contrary, the

---

[67] First Amendment of the U.S. Constitution prohibits the Congress from making a law that will abridge the freedom of speech or press. In this regard, see the Judgment of the Supreme Court of the United States, *Citizens United v. Federal Election Commission Appeal from the United States District Court for the District of Columbia*, No. 08–205, dated January 21, 2010.
[68] CM Rec(2003)4 on Common Rules against Corruption in the Funding of Political Parties and Electoral Campaigns, Preamble, Articles 1, 3 and 5.

intention was to protect subjective election rights, as without them the protection of human rights and freedoms in Europe would have remained incomplete.

1.2. Local Elections: The Charter of Local Self Government and the Convention on Participation of Foreigners in Public Life at Local Level

There is no true democracy, without democratically constituted bodies. This holds true also for local democracy. The very concept of local self-government, as the closest government to the citizens, demands direct, equal, universal, free and secret ballot for local authorities. In the CoE region, two legally-binding treaties contain election standards for local elections, thus supplementing the election standards for the legislature foreseen by the ECHR.

a. The Charter of Local Self-Government and Additional Protocol on the Right to Participate in the Affairs of a Local Authority

The Charter contains the essential characteristics and powers of local self-government in Europe.[69] The very concept of local self-government as a fundamental element of democracy requires free and fair elections.[70] The textual analysis of the Charter's Article 3 affirms that "free and fair elections" are indivisible from the concept of European local self-government.[71] Additional Protocol to the Charter considers universality, fairness and lawfulness as electoral principles. This Protocol reflects the evolution of election rights as individual rights in the context of local elections.

The election observation reports of the CLRAE provide the key to interpreting election standards in the local self-government context. The standard of "free and fair" is individualized and applied in light of the particular circumstances in view of the country's dynamics of democratic consolidation, as the CLRAE makes a political assessment of the country's situation. Taking into consideration its methodology, it has a limited power to observe the electoral processes, and thus cooperates and receives information from other election observers. The above facts do not deprive the election standards of their substance in the local elections context.

---

[69] Dimitrieva, Evropska Povelja o Lokalnoj Samoupravi, Implementacija Evropske Povelje o Lokalnoj Samoupravi u Republici Hrvatskoj, Simpozij Osijek (1998).
[70] Explanatory Memorandum of the Charter of Local Self-Government on Article 3.
[71] Preamble and Article 3 of the Charter.

The key electoral requirements underscored in CLRAE election observation reports remain a point of action for the state in question. The standard of "free and fair elections", as defined in the above-mentioned texts[72] and interpreted in the CLRAE election observation reports, entails the following political and legal desiderata for each phase of the electoral cycle:

Pre-election Phase

Political/Electoral System and Law: A minimal requirement for local self-government is directly elected collective bodies. The election refers to local councils or assemblies without legislative power, as designated by the ratifying states in line with Article 13 of the Charter. No such a requirement is in place for the selection of the mayors, thus indicating the lack of a European election standard in this regard.

Since local democracy is inconceivable without effective powers granted to the representatives of the people, the Charter is explicit in stating that in addition to the decision-making power, the power to hold accountable executive bodies (including mayors) is entrenched in the elected bodies.

The electoral system must enable the free election of local representatives under equal terms. The representatives must be elected by a similar number of votes. The equality of suffrage – the allocation of the same voting power does not prohibit positive action, aimed at a fair representation of minorities or women.

The formula for the election of minority representatives must be transparent, in order to avoid any manipulation with the minorities' vote. The requirement for the state parties to facilitate the exercise of election rights without unfair distinction, explains in greater detail the free and fair election standard. The above substantive provision reflects the European trend for greater inclusion of minorities and women through special measures, such as reserved seats for minorities, special candidates' lists or equitable representation on the list of candidates. The measures for greater inclusion of disadvantaged groups may be statutory, but they might also come as a result of the political parties' self-regulation.

---

[72] Charter of Local Self-Government, Article 3 and its Additional Protocol, Article 1 and Article 2.2(c). The Code of Good Practice in Electoral Matters is also used by the CLRAE to assess local and regional elections.

III. European Regional Organizations Developing Standards in the Election Field

The laws must be consistent and uniformly applied to avoid arbitrariness in the electoral processes. As long as the foreseeability and transparency principles in the laws are satisfied, the states may include categories of offices or activities deemed incompatible with the exercise of local representative office, entrenched in a statute or in a well-developed practice.

Voters: The active participation of the voters is crucial for the legitimacy and authority of the elected organ. The universality principle in the context of the European local election refers to the minimal election right in the Additional Protocol; the residents, nationals of the ratifying party must have the right to vote. The implementation limb of the Protocol, emphasizing the need for the introduction of special measures to facilitate voting for disadvantaged groups, is yet another manifestation of the universality principle.

The free expression of the will of voters is a complex criterion that foresees a number of important safeguards for voters, such as physical security, freedom from coercion and bribery, access to political programmes and information, physical access to polling stations and assistance to physically impaired persons. An updated and accurate voters' list is a must for having confidence in the election result as many electoral frauds are done by way of manipulating voters' lists. Voting rights can be limited or conditioned for the reasons of public safety or effective operation of democracy. Compliance with international obligations has been added in the exhaustive list of exceptions above.

Candidates: In addition to the universality principle, other desiderata for the candidates are quite straightforward. First, transparency in the process of candidates' nomination is an important safeguard of the passive election right. Second, their security must be ensured. Therefore, no government interventions, pressuring or intimidating candidates is allowed. Third, the candidates must be able to conduct free and visible campaigns, organize peaceful rallies and reach out to voters under the principle of equality of opportunity. Forth, without properly safeguarding the rights of all candidates, especially from the opposition, no plurality of real choice will exist. By the same token, although the passive election right is not absolute, there must not be unreasonable and impenetrable obstacles to the nomination of the candidates.

Financing and Electoral Campaign: The financing of the parties and electoral campaigns must meet the standards of fairness, transparency and responsibility for the competitors. This means that no administrative resources can be used or abused for the purpose of electoral campaigning.

It also means that the electoral campaign must be visible. In the visibility context, the media must not allow unfair advantages by giving higher discounts, or by not requesting a payment for their services. Furthermore they have a special obligation to distribute information in a responsible, balanced and transparent manner, without government involvement. Public electronic and print media must provide an accurate and fair coverage of all electoral options. The advertising space and billboards must be sufficient in number and placed in visible places.

Electoral Administration: All electoral bodies must be balanced in their composition, thus adhering to the principles of independence and impartiality. Their administrative and decision-making procedures must not be cumbersome, as they affect the legitimacy of the electoral process. For example, delays in declaring election results might raise suspicion of rigged elections.

Effective Legal Protection: Voters and candidates have to enjoy effective administrative protection of their rights in terms of voters' registration and deletion of voters who are ineligible, as well as in terms of candidates' nomination and alleged unequal treatment by the media. There must be effective criminal law remedies sanctioning all attempts to rig elections.

Election Day

Polling Stations: Properly managed and accessible polling stations are a key to a successful election. Therefore, first the assignment of the number of voters per polling station must be measured against the realistic time needed to cast a vote. Second, the polling station layout must simultaneously allow for a secret ballot and transparency about what has been happening inside the polling station. In particular, no unauthorized persons are allowed in or in the near vicinity of the polling stations. Police must not be present in the polling station, unless called by an authorized person. However, they must remain vigilant and accessible in case of security threats.

Electoral Materials: The ballot boxes and screens must be such fully to protect the secrecy of voting. Sensitive material, like counterfoils must be properly stored and packed, as that is one of the safeguards of the electoral integrity.

Voters: Instructions in the languages that voters understand must be visibly displayed together with the candidates' lists. The active election right is an individual right, hence no group or family voting is allowed.

Electoral Administration: The electoral administration at all levels must satisfy the requirements of independence, impartiality and professionalism. If political representatives are permitted, they must have balanced representation. The polling board members must be present during voting hours and the opening and closing of the polling station. All bodies, especially the polling boards, must be properly trained in all aspects of elections.

Effective Legal Protection: Violence, voters' manipulation, improper and non-transparent conduct of the voting procedure represent a cause for concern and must be prevented and effectively suppressed.

Post-election phase

Effective Resolution of Electoral Disputes: Electoral disputes must be resolved in an efficient, effective and an impartial manner, as post-election violence might occur as a result of a biased and ineffective system for the resolution of electoral disputes.

Mandate Entrusted to a Winning Candidate: The CLRAE requires transparent and accurate counting and tallying of the votes, and prompt display of the results. A successful election should result in a peaceful assumption of the office by a winning candidate.

When conducting a comparative analysis of the ECHR versus the Charter and its Additional Protocol, it is evident that both regulate only the election of collective bodies. While the

ECHR is applicable to the election of all kinds of legislatures, the latter only regulates local and regional elections of collective bodies without legislative power. With the Additional Protocol's entrance into force, both instruments approach elections as a manifestation of individual rights. However, the object of protection varies. Whereas the ECHR protects active and passive election rights viewed from the prism of a human rights and democracy doctrine, the Charter and the Protocol protect the local self-government concept. The latter approach to elections from the individual rights' perspective implicitly originates from the ever-increasing importance of the meaningful representation of various groups within society. Other principles (direct, equal, secret and free) are featured in the texts of both instruments, adjusted to the electoral context. Whereas the ECHR is interpreted by legal means by judges, the CLRAE employs more political criteria for the interpretation of "free and fair" standards, as its observers are elected officials. The point of convergence for understanding the common standard of a "free and fair elections" is the Code of Good Practice in Electoral Matters. Both the ECtHR and the CLRAE refer to it, when executing their electoral competencies.

All CoE members have now ratified the Charter, with Belgium not considering itself bound by Article 3 paragraph 2 of the Charter. Even with the interpretative statements of Spain and France, there is a European consensus on "free and fair" local elections as a key European value. Switzerland and Monaco, although not bound by the ECHR, have also ratified the Charter.

1.3. Electoral Guidelines: Code of Good Practice in Electoral Matters

The VC and the Council for Democratic Elections adopted the Code of Good Practice in Electoral Matters in 2002. It contains Guidelines and Explanatory Memorandum where a detailed account of the election standards based on the European electoral heritage has been set out. Although not legally-binding, the Code mentions two legally-binding instruments: the ICCPR and the ECHR, as the basis for its "hard core" principles.

The Code has categorized the election standards under the following tenets: universal, equal, free, secret, direct and regular elections. The legal form of the Code is rule-like and very precise in some domains, as it contains contemporary praxis based on the European electoral heritage. The free and fair electoral standard concerning each of the phases of the electoral cycle encompasses the following:

Pre-election Phase

Electoral System and Law: The principle of equality has been largely associated with the electoral system. The Code rules out different numbers of votes allocated to different groups or classes of people. Furthermore, the boundaries of the constituencies must take into account a number of criteria (population, residents, minors, registered voters and voters who actually cast their vote) in order to safeguard the equality of the voting power. Administrative, historic and geographical criteria may be taken into consideration when drawing the boundaries. The criteria are not only important when the boundaries are first drawn, but it is a continuous requirement needing a 10-year regular revision. Gerrymandering is prohibited.

Certain protection is afforded to minorities, as the boundaries must not be revised to their detriment, and their representatives might be included in the committees delimiting the boundaries, when necessary. Drawing the boundaries of the constituencies to allow minorities to be better represented, is neither required nor prohibited.

The direct election principle does not exceed the requirements with respect to the election of at least one chamber of the legislature and of local councils foreseen in the ECHR and the Charter of Local-Self Government.

Election rules must be stable and included in the statute if not in the constitution. This is a condition, *sine qua non,* for holding free and fair elections. They are not amenable to amendments at least one year before elections.

Voters and Candidates: The universality principle applies to the voters, as well as to the candidates. All the afore-mentioned requirements are captured regarding: a) limitations of election rights (age, nationality, residence, immigrants); and b) deprivation of election rights (lawfulness, proportionality and the reasons for deprivation: mental incapacity and serious criminal offence). The novelty in this regard is the clarification that the scrutiny applicable to the deprivation of the passive election right is less strict compared to the scrutiny applicable to the deprivation of the active election right. The two reasons for deprivation, mental incapacity and a serious criminal offence, require a court decision. The only element that is missing compared to the requirements from other CoE instruments is the individualization of the decision, depriving individuals of their election rights. Furthermore, the Code requires disfranchisement only for a serious criminal offence. However, there is no definition of what constitutes a serious criminal offence. Hence, not all election-related criminal offences may qualify, as not all of them fall within the definition of a serious crime in terms of punishment, e.g. election-related minor offences. The temporal dimension of the deprivation of election rights based on conviction, has not been explicitly mentioned anywhere. The only inference in this regard can be made based on the principle of proportionality.

The voters' list standards have been clearly set out in comparison to the previously examined documents. The requirement of a transparent voters' list is prominent. However, it should be clearly stated that the transparency of the voters' list should not run counter to the right to privacy.

The individual candidates' registration has been addressed in great detail by lowering the number of the signatures required, and foreseeing clear and precise rules. On the other side of the coin, the electoral deposit rules requires a "reasonable amount", and a deposit reimbursement, when a certain threshold of popularity is passed. Transparency and access to information regarding candidates have been clearly enunciated, being a key requirement of pluralist election.

Funding and Media: Equality of opportunity, as the "third face" of the equality principle, is applicable to the protection of the rights of parties and candidates in terms of financing and media. Whereas equality of opportunity is compulsory for access to public media, public funding and the organization of the electoral campaign, the states can choose its form, i.e., strict or proportional equality of opportunity.

Minimal access to private media, as foreseen by the Code, can hardly fall within the principle of equality of opportunity, despite being counterbalanced with the limits on spending and transparency. Access to private media on unequal basis can distort the fairness principle. Private media are owned by the parties, candidates and their supporters. Not only does the ruling party have better access to private media, but it may also abuse the state institutions and interfere with the private media critical of it. Therefore, the above minimal requirement must be read together with the equality of opportunity in the election campaign and in financing, in order to discern its true meaning. Minimal access to private media is construed as a further requirement relating to private media, and not as an exception to the already formulated equality of opportunities' rules.

Electoral Administration: Regardless of the model chosen (independent, governmental or mixed) the impartiality and independence of the electoral administration must be ensured, *inter alia,* by setting it up as a permanent body with clear and transparent decision-making.

Effective Legal Remedies: Effective judicial remedies must be available for voter registration and the cleaning-up of voters' list, as well as for the candidates' nomination. Any intimidation, pressure or abuse of the state apparatus in order to violate the voters' freedom to form an opinion must be sanctioned.

Adequate legal remedies must be available in case of tampering with electoral results, even to the voters, when forming a certain quorum. When elections are annulled, they must be repeated. This rule applies even when the electoral result has not been affected by the annulled votes in a polling station, as the voters in such a case will be effectively deprived of their right to vote. In any case, the electoral results where a fraud was discovered, should be annulled. Such votes must not be counted, especially if the allocation of public funds is connected with the number of the votes gained.

An adequate legal remedy is also indispensable in case of electoral campaign manipulations. Although lacking in the Code, the monitoring of media coverage and electoral campaign expenses is important in terms of prevention, as well as for the effective investigation and prosecution of such offences.

An effective legal remedy must have short and realistic deadlines, allowing a thorough examination of complaints and appeals. Short deadlines may be a good excuse for a superficial examination of the appeals and complaints. However, a hearing of both parties is required by the Code.

The Code does not go in detail about the types of sanctions. Not all sanctions have a deterrent effect. It might be more in the interest of the parties to pay a fine as long as they are winning elections.

<u>Election Day</u>

Voters: Voters need simple and clear instructions about the voting, also in the minorities' languages.

Voting procedures and electoral materials: While, non-polling station procedures may be available to safeguard the universality of the vote for various voters' groups, they must not override the secrecy, equality and free expression of the voters. The sensitive electoral material (e.g. electoral slips) must be properly safeguarded.

The equality of vote principle prohibits multiple voting. Family voting is strictly prohibited, regardless of the tradition or prevailing local culture, since it effectively deprives, mostly women, from their voting rights.

The voting procedures must be transparent, lawful and fraud impermeable. The principle of transparency is also applicable with respect to the counting. The practice in the Balkan states (Macedonia, Bosnia and Herzegovina) was to lock the door after the voting had ended for safety reasons, with the electoral and party observers kept inside. However, no media have access as nobody can go out or come in as long as the results are in the process of being counted. Transparency is ensured by posting the results in front of the polling station. It appears that this practice might satisfy the minimal requirement for transparency, as long as there is a real security threat. A secret counting of votes runs counter to the principles of "free and fair elections". The transparency requirement should also continue to be observed at all levels of the electoral administration hierarchy, including during votes' tabulation.

Just like with other international instruments, the secrecy of the ballot is guaranteed not only while casting the vote, but also afterwards, as no one should compel another person to disclose their favorite candidate. No stamping or signing of the ballots is allowed when handed over to the voters, as it might be possible to identify the voter's ballot afterwards.

<u>The Post-Election Phase</u>

The equality of outcome in terms of, for example, equal representation of men and women is not foreseen as a requirement in the Code. It also does not require a parity of sexes in the candidates' nomination, or any other special measures to increase the participation of women in public life.

Periodic elections ensure that the elected collective body reflects the will of the electors. For the legislature, such term should not exceed 5 years.

While detailing some of the European election principles, the Code does not devote much attention to regulation of the election campaign. In particular, the print media is not explicitly mentioned anywhere. Electoral campaign financing is also scarcely mentioned. Whereas it may be that the GRECO covers electoral campaign financing and there is a CoE publication on political parties and electoral campaign financing, the question arises as to why this part is barely tackled, when almost all of the most difficult problems in the West or East relating to elections are connected with the electoral campaign.

Although adopted almost 12 years after the fall of socialism, the Code mentions that different approaches might be considered, depending on the democratic tradition, relative to election issues. Due to different democratic traditions, it might happen that some of the suggestions in the Code are not the best solution for a particular country. As an example, the Code suggests to have at least one judge and the most important political party representatives appointed to the central election commission with the aim of ensuring its impartiality. However, in some countries, such a composition had to be changed due to allegations of partiality of the judges. In addition, the political party representatives voted along party lines, effectively taking away the right to appeal to the parties not represented in the commission.

The issue of effective compliance with the Code and the follow-up to the VC's reviews of election legislation opinions remain open. To some extent, they are ensured by other international organizations, including the OSCE/ODIHR and OSCE field operations. The quest for effective compliance and a harmonized approach towards European election standards is one of the reasons for PACE's Recommendation 1595 (2003) to the CM for the

Code to be transposed into a convention. However, the idea regarding an election convention was not followed through.

1.4. Financing of Electoral Campaign: Group of States against Corruption

The CoE instrument containing the most comprehensive rules about electoral campaign financing is the Committee of Ministers' Recommendation (2003) 4 on Common Rules against Corruption in the Funding of Political Parties and Electoral Campaigns. The Recommendation focuses on transparent electoral funding, donation limits, proper financial reporting, audit and effective punishment in connection with all types of elections (parliamentary, presidential, regional and local elections). Its aim is to approximate the respective legislation of the CoE member states and contribute towards a successful fight against corruption in the CoE region.

Although the Recommendation is legally non-binding, it reflects the political will of all members of the CoE. Therefore, it cannot be considered declaratory only. It is a type of soft law. In particular, the Recommendation contains very precise rules regarding the funding of electoral candidates' and elected officials' activities. In addition, there is an institutionalized and systematic follow-up to the Recommendation by GRECO. This body is mandated to monitor the compliance of the CoE member states with the anti-corruption standards enunciated in the afore-mentioned Recommendation and the Guiding Principle for the Fight against Corruption no. 15.

Under the Recommendation, the CoE member states are required to adopt national rules reflecting common standards for combating corruption in relation to electoral campaign financing. The common measures for fighting corruption in relation to electoral campaign financing flow from the following principles:

1. Fairness

State support to political parties is allowed, when clearly prescribed by law. However, it must be allocated on an equitable basis in line with objective and reasonable criteria. The above-mentioned criteria also cover indirect public funding in terms of free air time, use of premises and tax exemptions.

State and public enterprises must not make donations. The obligation also extends to companies controlled by the state. The obligation is less intense in the case of state (public entities) contracted companies, whose donations may be strictly regulated or limited.

Conflicts of interest regarding the use and allocation of state resources must be avoided, when the aim is to prevent and suppress corruption. Thus, occupants of political offices and public servants must not use public resources for the benefit of their own or a party candidates' electoral campaign.

For proper application of the respective rules, there must be effective procedures to detect and punish any circumvention of the donation limits. Thus, the above rules are also applicable to the donations made to the entities connected to political parties, e.g., research institutes.[73]

As the states' law and practice differ regarding funding by corporations, the Recommendation does not foresee a prohibition on donations to political parties by corporations. The avoidance of influence on political parties and politicians by "big money" is regulated via the imposition of a limit on donations.

As a comment, the fairness principle not only safeguards equal opportunity for political parties to win the elections, but it also protects them from undue pressures and interference with their autonomy. Since large contracts worth millions often represent a cause of bribery of high-ranking politicians, and considering that interference with internal politics may come from foreign entities, the Recommendation requires foreign donations to be prohibited, strictly regulated or limited.

The majority of components which make up the fairness requirement are found in the first part of the Recommendation. This part is specifically tailored to the sources of funding of political parties, and applies, *mutatis mutandis,* to electoral campaign financing. Such an approach leaves a gap in the regulation of the external sources of electoral campaigns. For example, there is no explicit mention of public funding of individual election candidates,

---

[73] See for example, GRECO Evaluation Report on Serbia, 3E (2010) p. 22, as well as on Romania 1 F (2010) p. 36.

which might put them at a disadvantage vis-à-vis political parties. In principle, Article 8 applies to all electoral candidates, and not only to party candidates. Furthermore, if restrictions apply to individual candidates, by analogy the advantages should apply to them also. However, the requirements for donation records or for disclosure of accounts are again made explicitly applicable solely to the political parties. In conclusion, it is unclear to what extent the individual electoral candidates' funding in terms of obligations and benefits is covered by the above Recommendation.

By the same token, the relationship between the funding of political parties and electoral campaign has been left unexplored, although it opens a space for circumventing the main aim of the Recommendation: the fight against corruption. In particular, different states differently regulate electoral campaign financing and the sources of funds. Immediately, a question pops up how to detect and account for funding of electoral campaign activities, which are not part of the electoral campaign of a candidate. It does not need to be a local committee of the electoral party, it can be a private company doing it. Such an "open space" in the electoral campaign financing may result in circumventing the upper limit of the allowed expenditures or donations. The GRECO, in its evaluation reports related to this topic, attempts to mitigate these consequences by recommending that support and expenditure pass through an election agent and election accounts, as far as possible.[74] Likewise, it expects no electoral campaign expenditures to be made outside of the electoral campaign period, as that represents a violation of the electoral campaign rules.[75]

2. Transparency

All sources of income used for the electoral campaign, such as donations (monetary or in-kind or any other advantaged bestowed on a political party), electoral candidate personal contributions, party membership fees,[76] loans and sponsorships, as well as their nature and value, must be duly recorded in the books and reported to the competent body. The lowest disclosure standard is identification of the source for all donations and the type of the donation exceeding a certain amount.[77] Anonymous donations are prohibited.[78] It is further

---

[74] See, among others, Evaluation Report on Ukraine 1F (2011) p. 33.
[75] GRECO Evaluation Report on Serbia 3E (2010) p. 22.
[76] GRECO Evaluation Report on the Russian Federation, 6E (2011) p. 39.
[77] GRECO Evaluation Report on Switzerland, 4F (2011) p. 21.

required that donations of private companies be disclosed to the shareholders or other individual members of a legal entity, thus deterring any "suspicious" donations.

Likewise a detailed record of all expenditures should be kept.[79] The recommendation encompasses direct and indirect expenditure for each and every political party, each list of candidates and each candidate. Evenmore so, the accounting requirement includes local party bodies and other entities included in the campaign. A standardized format is recommended for auditing.[80]

The donation and expenditure commitments are valid for coalitions as accounting should be given for each member of the coalition and each electoral candidate individually, according to the GRECO evaluation reports.

While the annual reporting requirement refers to giving access to the accounts to a supervisory authority, the disclosure requirement confers the right of the public[81] to get regular access at least annually to political parties' accounts, or to a summary of them.[82]

The above rules are much easier to put into legislation than to implement properly. For example, there are objections to disclosing donors of opposition parties who fear that they might suffer disadvantages regarding their business activities, e.g., winning a public contract or not receiving needed permissions. In addition, the reporting and disclosure requirements might not be fully implemented by their subjects in the absence of an effective and impartial monitoring and investigative system.

Last, but not least clear and coherent laws go hand-in-hand with the transparency requirement.[83]

3. Accountability

An independent monitoring[84] in respect of the accounts of the political parties and expenses, their presentation and publication is a condition, *sine qua non,* to ensure the fairness and

---

[78] GRECO Evaluation Reports on Albania 7E (2009) p. 24, Austria 3E, (2011) p. 24 and Italy 7F (2011) p. 34.
[79] GRECO Evaluation Reports on Azerbaijan 2E, (2010) p. 29 and Monaco 5F (2011) p. 15.
[80] GRECO Evaluation Report on Portugal 6F (2010) p. 25.
[81] GRECO Evaluation Report on Serbia 3E (2010) p. 22 and Russian Federation 6E (2011). p. 39.
[82] GRECO Evaluation Report on Romania 1F (2010) p. 36.
[83] GRECO Evaluation Report on Belgium 8F and on Ukraine 1F (2011) p. 33.
[84] GRECO Evaluation Report on Romania, 1F (2010) p. 36.

lawfulness of the system.[85] The mechanism for combating corruption in the politics should also encompass specialized and trained bodies with investigative and sanctioning powers. Sanctions must be sufficient to demonstrate that breaking the rules does not pay off.[86] Donors should also be made liable for breaching electoral financing rules.

Accountability is the biggest issue regarding electoral campaign financing.[87] While auditing might be done properly by a special accounting body, the breach of electoral campaign financing rules might not receive a satisfactory follow-up in terms of prosecution and punishment, thus perpetuating impunity. The prosecution part is even made more difficult knowing that the subject of the proceedings may be high ranking officials or party members who have abused the rules for the sake of the party, and thus expect to be shielded by it. Other problems that might occur include selective targeting only of the members of the opposition. A fine line must not be crossed between accountability and the abuse of the judicial apparatus with the purpose of threatening and coercing the opposition.

1.5. Observations on the Council of Europe Election Standards

It is undeniable that there are CoE standards in the election field. It would have been inconceivable for this European organization to observe elections and afford legal protection to individuals, in absence of such standards.

The CoE standard of "free and fair elections" has been re-conceptualized time and again since the 1952 Protocol no. 1 to the ECHR. While the treaties represent the most authoritative source of election standards, political and expert documents capture in greater detail controversial topics such as electoral financing. Regardless if there was a strategy from the outset to deepen and geographically extend the election standards step-by-step, or that happened by a random choice, the fact remains that more and more election standards are emerging from the CoE bodies.

---

[85] On the requirement for effective monitoring of election campaign financing see (among others) the GRECO Evaluation Report on Albania 7E, Transparency on Party Funding (2009) p. 24.
[86] GRECO Evaluation Report on Azerbaijan 2E (2010) p. 29.
[87] On the requirement for independent audit, see GRECO Evaluation Report on the Russian Federation, 6E (2011) p. 39.

Considering that the CoE standards come from a variety of sources, there is always a risk of dissonance among them. However, the electoral principles of secret, direct, free, periodic, universal and equal elections cross-cut the boundaries of various instruments and mandates. The points of convergence among various standards from the election field are clearly enunciated in the Code of Good Practice in Electoral Matters. Of course, the most important point of convergence which holds the election standards together across CoE are its member-states, which have consented to those standards. They must harmonize their practices while implementing them. In particular, the prevailing majority of the CoE member states have ratified the ECHR P-1 and the Charter of Local Self-Government. The Code of Good Conduct in Electoral Matters represents codification of the electoral rules and best practices at the European level. It follows that a prevailing majority of the CoE members are legally bound and value the same principles applicable in the election arena.

There is no need to come up with yet another exhaustive list of election standards unifying all CoE standards. The latter cannot be perceived as merely an amalgam of various standards. On the contrary, each instrument and its respective praxis, provide guidance that is categorized on the bases of the type of elections and the specific electoral standard.

No CoE document attempts to innovate in building electoral architecture. While the base of the construction remains the same, the liberal approach used to interpret them means stricter responsibility for states in implementing those standards. Although meaningful representation in decision-making has been acknowledged as a provider of peace and stability and protector of democracy, it has not been explicitly included as a desired electoral outcome. The CoE should make an attempt to conceptualize the right to meaningful representation as an electoral standard of outcome, thus moving away from the minimalist concept of liberal democracy.

2. OSCE

At the European level, the OSCE is vested with a leading role with respect to election observations. The OSCE mandate relates to the protection of peace and security in Europe based on a broad concept, which also deals with protection of democracy and human rights.

III. European Regional Organizations Developing Standards in the Election Field

Since elections are: "a structural component of a democratic society", all OSCE participating states adhere to the OSCE commitment to hold "free and fair" elections.

The OSCE commitments are a product of negotiations and agreement between the representatives of the participating states.[88] They are not legally-binding. In this context, it should be mentioned that the OSCE participating states have not yet agreed even to a constituting treaty, thus indicating that a legally-binding document in terms of elections is not high on the agenda of the OSCE participating states.

Still, it cannot be said that the OSCE commitments are just simple recommendations, because of the following:

First, they ensue from a political process and are agreed upon by all high representatives of the participating states. The methodology used for their elaboration and their endorsement by the OSCE participating states gives them a specific political value, meaning that they represent political obligation for the OSCE participating states. Besides, the OSCE is vested with a norm-setting capacity, as reaffirmed in 2005.[89]

Second, the content of the existing commitments is precise and detailed, which indicates a consensus among the OSCE participating states regarding their implementation. Third, the participating states have made a promise regarding particular follow-up on their implementation in good faith. Lastly, the OSCE commitments are a manifestation of the UN obligations set out in the UDHR and ICCPR in support of "a global consensus for democracy [that] emerged in the 1990s".[90] In view of the above, the OSCE commitments are politically-binding, thus belonging to the realm of soft law.[91]

The principle of multiparty democracy based on free, periodic and genuine elections was mentioned for the first time as a common value of the participating states in 1990, with the

---

[88] OSCE Human Dimension Commitments, Vol. 1, Thematic Compilation, 3rd edition (2011) p. xvi at <http:/www.osce.org>.
[89] The OSCE Ministerial Council Decision No. 17/05.
[90] OSCE/ODIHR, Existing Commitments for Democratic Elections in OSCE Participating States (2003) pp. 7 and 11 at <http:/www.osce.org>.
[91] Manton, Knoll, Monitoring within the OSCE Office for Democratic Institutions and Human Rights (ODIHR) at <http:/www.osce.org>.

fall of the socialist system. The participating states have declared their commitment to pluralist and representative democracy based on free and regular elections, separation of powers and distinction between the state and political parties. The right of the people to take part in the governing of their own country is affirmed as a common value. The OSCE has followed the same eclectic approach used for other commitments, while developing electoral commitments. Namely, they are contained in a number of documents, which have taken a form of summit declarations, ministerial council decisions or a charter in the political sense of the word.[92] The OSCE electoral tree, with each of its branches representing a commitment for holding free and fair elections, is deeply rooted in the 1990 Copenhagen Document of the Conference on the Human Dimension of the CSCE (the Copenhagen Document).[93]

---

[92] The OSCE electoral commitments are spread in the following texts: the 1990 Copenhagen Document, the 1990 Bonn Document, the 1990 Paris Document, the 1991 Moscow Document, the 1991 Geneva Document, the 1994 Budapest Document, the 1996 Lisbon Document, the 1999 Istanbul Document , the 2002 Porto Document, the 2003 Maastricht Document, the 2006 Brussels Document and the 2010 Astana Document.

[93] Its Annex 1 reads as follows:

"(6) The participating States declare that the will of the people, freely and fairly expressed through periodic and genuine elections, is the basis of the authority and legitimacy of all government. The participating States will accordingly respect the right of their citizens to take part in the governing of their country, either directly or through representatives freely chosen by them through fair electoral processes. They recognize their responsibility to defend and protect, in accordance with their laws, their international human rights obligations and their international commitments, the democratic order freely established through the will of the people against the activities of persons, groups or organizations that engage in or refuse to renounce terrorism or violence aimed at the overthrow of that order or of that of another participating State.

(7) To ensure that the will of the people serves as the basis of the authority of government, the participating States will

(7.1) - hold free elections at reasonable intervals, as established by law;

(7.2) - permit all seats in at least one chamber of the national legislature to be freely contested in a popular vote;

(7.3) - guarantee universal and equal suffrage to adult citizens;

(7.4) - ensure that votes are cast by secret ballot or by equivalent free voting procedure, and that they are counted and reported honestly with the official results made public;

(7.5) - respect the right of citizens to seek political or public office, individually or as representatives of political parties or organizations, without discrimination;

(7.6) - respect the right of individuals and groups to establish, in full freedom, their own political parties or other political organizations and provide such political parties and organizations with the necessary legal guarantees to enable them to compete with each other on a basis of equal treatment before the law and by the authorities;

(7.7) - ensure that law and public policy work to permit political campaigning to be conducted in a fair and free atmosphere in which neither administrative action, violence nor intimidation bars the parties and the candidates from freely presenting their views and qualifications, or prevents the voters from learning and discussing them or from casting their vote free of fear of retribution;

(7.8) - provide that no legal or administrative obstacle stands in the way of unimpeded access to the media on a non-discriminatory basis for all political groupings and individuals wishing to participate in the electoral process;

(7.9) - ensure that candidates who obtain the necessary number of votes required by law are duly installed in office and are permitted to remain in office until their term expires or is otherwise brought to an end in a manner that is regulated by law in conformity with democratic parliamentary and constitutional procedures.

(8) The participating States consider that the presence of observers, both foreign and domestic, can enhance the electoral process for States in which elections are taking place. They therefore invite observers from any other

Its wording connotes that the OSCE participating states are committed to safeguarding the sustainability of the democratic order. Since that is intrinsically linked with representative democracy, only free and fair elections can represent a basis for the legitimacy and authority of the government in the OSCE region. Thus, it appears that the requirement to defend democratic government against any violent attempts at overthrow is interrelated with the sustainability of the democratic order. It has already happened in modern European history that non-democratic governments have been elected. Therefore, the above "defense" commitment has been carved in light of the international and OSCE human rights protection instruments. If the contrary was the case, other OSCE human dimension commitments might be endangered by a democratically elected, but a non-democratic government. It is inferred from the Copenhagen Document that the sustainability of the democratic order has been conceived as one of the outputs of the OSCE commitments, which strives to protect and enhance peace on European soil. Therefore, the 1991 specific commitment for the support of an elected government against coup d'état, must be interpreted in line with the requirement to protect the democratic order and other human dimension commitments undertaken by the OSCE participating states.

For democratic order to be established, paragraph 6 of Annex I of the Copenhagen Document requires a government to be formed on the basis of the free and fair expression of the will of the people. To attain the purpose of holding genuine elections, the Document has taken the approach of respect for the election rights of individuals. Thus, governments must take care that each of their citizens are able to cast his or her vote in a free and fair manner, and not only with respect to elections of legislature. However, this requirement does not limit the OSCE/ODIHR electoral observation and assistance mandate only to elections of the legislature.

The content analysis of paragraphs 6-8 of the Copenhagen Document, divulge the following principles of the electoral model applicable in the OSCE region:[94]

CSCE participating States and any appropriate private institutions and organizations who may wish to do so to observe the course of their national election proceedings, to the extent permitted by law. They will also endeavour to facilitate similar access for election proceedings held below the national level. Such observers will undertake not to interfere in the electoral proceedings."

[94] OSCE Human Dimension Commitments, Vol. 1, Thematic Compilation, 3rd edition (2011) p. xxii at <http:/www.osce.org>.

1) Elections must be free in all their dimensions. In a nutshell, this means that electoral rights are universal: voters are able to make their choice freely, while the candidates' nomination is not burdened by arbitrary requirements. It also means that the media and electoral contestants can freely spread political information. Since human rights translate the freedom of human beings into concrete terms, the right to political association and to peaceful assembly remain the essence of free elections.

2) Fairness, as an electoral principle, cannot be separated from the non-discrimination commitment. Its architecture is based on the following pillars: the equal treatment of candidates and media on one hand, and the secrecy of vote on the other hand. Since, the fairness principle is closely linked with electoral integrity, the election observation is included in the OSCE commitments.

3) Elections must be genuine, meaning that electoral processes are carried out in a manner that ensures that their outcome reflects the true choice of the people. This principle requires that counting, tabulation and reporting of the results is done transparently, honestly and in public. The electoral outcome must be respected, meaning that the winning candidates must be installed and occupy the office until the expiration of their term.[95] Regular elections go hand-in-hand with government respect for the will of the people as the source of sovereignty.

Subsequent OSCE documents have gradually added complementary electoral commitments. Yet the principles set out above remain unchanged. With reference to the "fairness principle", states must curtail impunity in electoral fraud cases, as it endangers stability in the OSCE region. Under the same principle, the requirements for equal rights with respect to access to media and holding rallies in the electoral context were made explicit. Furthermore, the "free election principle" cannot be fully observed without full enjoyment of election rights for refugees. Hence, it was set out as a requirement, along with full respect for the voting rights of minorities. Special attention was also devoted to the enhancement of the participation of

---

[95] Ghebali, Debating Election and Election Monitoring Standard at the OSCE: Between Technical Needs And Politicization (2006) p. 217.

women in political life and the prohibition of family voting, which *de facto* disenfranchises women.[96]

The Copenhagen document regulates restrictions to the above rights by making reference to other international commitments, like the ICCPR and the UDHR, and to the principles of lawfulness and proportionality. Derogations in case of public emergency are based on lawfulness, proportionality and non-discrimination, in line with the Siracusa principles.[97]

While respect for minorities' voting rights is included in the OSCE commitments in general terms, they have been largely supplemented by the Lund Recommendations on Effective Participation of National Minorities in Public Life (the Recommendations). The latter are not commitments in the sense that they have been agreed upon by the Heads of States or Ministers. Nevertheless, they are worth mentioning, as they represent one of the most effective tools for better inclusion of national minorities in decision-making, without having to undergo the process of formal ratifications. Starting from the premise that participation in public affairs is a human right, the Lund Recommendations propose concrete measures and bodies at all governance levels, respectively. Elections are especially tackled as one of the modalities for facilitating political inclusion of this specially-targeted group in democratic decision-making. In this context, states should take special care to ensure freedom from discrimination and freedom of political association, as well as types of electoral systems and boundaries of electoral districts, which should facilitate minority representation and their influence, in addition to effective judicial remedies (e. g., against decisions such as demarcation of electoral districts).

Since OSCE participating states are committed to the implementation of the OSCE commitments, OSCE/ODIHR provides electoral support to them in the form of election observation. The observers focus and report on the patterns extracted during the election observation, and do not monitor or provide redress for violations of individual election rights. ODIHR issues findings that are impartial, as well as recommendations of a concrete nature.

---

[96] See the 1991 Moscow Document (paragraph 40.8), the 1999 Istanbul Document and, in particular, the Sofia 2004 Annex: Action Plan for the Promotion of Gender Equality.
[97] United Nations, Economic and Social Council, U.N. Sub-Commission on Prevention of Discrimination and Protection of Minorities, Siracusa Principles on the Limitation and Derogation of Provisions in the International Covenant on Civil and Political Rights, Annex, UN Doc E/CN.4/1984/4 (1984).

In the most striking cases of electoral irregularities, ODIHR clearly states that key OSCE commitments were not met.

All participating states, except for the Holy See, have undergone ODIHR's electoral scrutiny despite limited funds. Azerbaijan was the first country in 1995, whereby the whole of elections were monitored and not only the conduct during Election Day. Since 2002, upon governments' invitation, election assessment missions have been deployed to long-standing democracies, such as the Netherlands, Italy, the UK, and France. According to ODIHR, in the countries west of Vienna, the electorate had confidence in the process, unlike the countries east of Vienna where some times large numbers of observers were requested to ensure the integrity of elections.

In some of the countries where the ODIHR has deployed election observation missions, there is no consistent improvement trend. On the contrary, it seems they have been acting as "bad pupils", as one more or less positive assessment is followed in the next elections with an assessment indicating trends of negative practices and election irregularities.[98] It might be true that the assessment of the elections by ODIHR takes into consideration the particular circumstances, i.e., if the elections were organized right after armed conflict, it is more likely that any such assessment will be more positive, put in the context of stopped violence and a brokered peace agreement. Nonetheless, according to the countries' trends throughout the years, some of the countries have never managed to make a "break-through" and organize free and fair elections, in spite of numerous ODIHR reports and recommendations. This is especially true for some countries situated in South-Eastern Europe and the Caucasus. An increase in the number, type and gravity of electoral irregularities over the years indicates a dangerous trend for certain European countries. Actually, it indicates the level and sustainability of democracy in a particular country. If such a trend persists in a number of countries from the same region, it provides an indicator of the level and sustainability of democracy for the whole region. A plethora of electoral irregularities in a certain region reduces the probability of holding free and fair elections in a country from that region. The good news is that elections are seldom accompanied by physical violence in the European

---

[98] See the Annex depicting the most re-occurring and wide-spread irregularities in the OSCE participating states.

countries. From ODIHR reports it is clear that long-standing democracies can still benefit from an impartial technical eye examining their electoral framework and practice.

Electoral problems trends show the following:

First, deficient legislation is a wide-spread problem. The laws may contain restrictions on freedoms of expression, assembly, political association and the passive election right, which are incompatible with the European standards. The applicable legislation may be ambiguous and full of lacunae, which makes possible differences in interpretation and inconsistent application. Furthermore, the legislation may not provide for a clear division of competencies between various bodies and courts, which results in a lack of proper application of the law. Sometimes the competent bodies choose not to implement the legislation fully. Such conduct is equal to arbitrariness, since the law is not respected.

Second, a lack of effective remedy is another wide-spread electoral irregularity. Its occurrence goes hand in hand with partial and incompetent EMBs. It appears that the bodies responsible for the lawfulness of the process cannot cope with all the challenges. The problems in this respect may be caused by the model for the EMBs' elections, if its members are elected by the biggest parties, appointing their "party soldiers"; because the officials are subject to threats and intimidation; or due to a lack of time, knowledge or competence how to investigate and process complaints. In many countries, the ODIHR observers have noticed a failure of these bodies to operate in a transparent manner, which raises doubts about the lawfulness of their work. A lack of accountability of the EMBs indicates a weak legal culture and disrespect for the rule of law, although it is a cornerstone of a democratic society.

A lack of access to judicial remedy for a number of violations of election rights, especially during the pre-election phase, is yet another example of a legislative deficiency (e.g., against media-related discriminatory practices, or against insufficient financial reporting).

Third, inaccurate voters' lists represent a problem in the majority of countries. The problem is compounded further by a lack of effective remedy for voters who do not appear on the voters' lists, and who are thus are effectively disenfranchised. Or, phantom votes were detected (e.g. dead people voting), which influence the outcome of election.

Fourth, a suppression of the opposition continues to be a problem in the OSCE region. Problems range from restrictions in candidacy and restricted access to media and biased media, to state apparatus' intimidations, and even incarceration of opposition figures. When there are substantial campaign restrictions, a wide-spread media bias and an intimidating environment, it is difficult to speak about genuine elections. In particular, a low-key campaign results in uninformed voters who may not feel that they can cast the ballot freely. By the same token, campaign financing with no ceilings results in unequal chances, usually of opposition candidates, to compete in elections. Further unfair advantage is gained by abusing state and administrative resources, thus indicating an amalgam between party and state resources. The above- mentioned irregularities occur with a frequency ranging between high and medium for the examined years.[99]

Fifth, violations of election procedures continue to be a challenge for a number of OSCE participating states. In many instances, observers noticed that the procedures set out by law were not observed, especially relating to effective legal remedies and counting and tabulation procedures. Interference with counting and tabulation procedures is becoming a more and more popular way of fixing election results, thereby assuring fraudulent electoral victory. In addition, family, proxy, group and multiple voting continue to violate the right to freely and secretly cast a ballot. Such irregularities cannot be considered as minor, or as part of a tradition. In fact, they indicate that women and vulnerable minorities (e.g. Roma) are mostly deprived of their voting rights. When voters are intimidated or bribed, then the electoral administration is also failing to discharge its duties properly. Transparency of the voting, counting and tallying procedures has been also raised with respect to new voting technologies.

Sixth, impunity or selective justice represents one of the biggest problems in the OSCE region. It gives a signal that committing election-related offences pays off. Sometimes such convicts even receive a presidential pardon. As a rule, election-related offences are committed for the benefit of an election candidate and political party, and are thought through and committed by a group. Impunity indicates that competent, effective and impartial prosecution and judiciary is lacking in a number of OSCE states. Proper sanctioning policy

---

[99] See Annex.

serving as a deterrent in this regard is another facet of the problem of lack of effective remedies in the OSCE area.

Last but not least, the negative trend of inequitable representation of women continues. Minorities, as a vulnerable group, continue not to be sufficiently included in elections as candidates. Additionally, states are not sufficiently engaged in providing information in the minority language or in facilitating the vote of minorities in case of illiteracy.

The bigger picture of electoral conduct in Europe demonstrates that in certain countries (or even regions) political actors, in absence of enlightened knowledge of democracy, still adhere to the old Machiavellian strategy, in order to win the prize of power! Electoral irregularities create a vicious circle, where the electoral rights of the citizens are not respected and no irregularities can be corrected at a later stage. The end result is a lack of accountability and public confidence, and eventually deficient democracy. The statements that there is no political will for holding free and fair elections means that the power in such societies is kept with a small elite, and that a separation of powers, the rule of law or human rights protection is deficient. Flawed elections indicate that in the particular country, democracy has not taken permanent hold, but its social system has taken a different shape, maybe more in a form of an oligarchy. The futility of efforts to restore democracy in such cases may undermine confidence in it, leading to a public perception of democracy as "the word for something that does not exist".[100]

2.1. From Commitments to Fully Fledged Election Standards

The following specific election standards are deduced for each of the phases of the electoral cycle by using the OSCE commitments extracted from the election-related documents and the ODIHR election observation and assessment reports as a secondary source.

Pre-election Phase

---

[100] Popper, Unended Quest: An Intellectual Autobiography (Macedonian, published by Magor) (1999) p. 9.

III. European Regional Organizations Developing Standards in the Election Field

Electoral system and law: The basis of the OSCE commitments is connected with democracy as a sole system of governance in the OSCE region. Voters are guaranteed at least one electoral opportunity, i.e., an election of one chamber of the legislature. Whereas the commitments do not foresee a special electoral system, it must be shaped in accordance with the assumed OSCE election-related commitments. The obligations for elections to reflect the free will of the people, and to be periodic must be enshrined in the law.

As a rule, the electoral law must be clear and coherent, with the changes in the legislation adopted well before elections.[101]

Election observation: The election observation system of the participating states has been scrutinized by election observation missions, which require access to be granted by law to local and international observers, to all phases of the electoral process.[102] Since in all OSCE participating states there have been electoral observation or assessment activities, it follows that election observation has become a norm in the OSCE area.

Voters: The principle of universality is underlined in the OSCE commitments, along with the principle of equality, i.e., all adult citizens must have the same election rights without a distinction on the grounds of property, gender, social status or any other ground relating to his or her personal status. Boundaries must be drawn to give equal weight of each vote to the extent possible. Along these lines, the electoral boundaries should be drawn in a way so as to favor the representation of minorities.[103] In view of the above requirements, the accuracy of the electoral rolls is always scrutinized by the ODIHR observers, while due consideration is given to the personal data protection requirement.[104]

Candidates: The principles of universality and equality also apply with respect to the passive election right, i.e., the right to seek office either individually or in a group. This right may be

---

[101] OSCE/ODIHR Final Election Observation Reports on Belarussion 2012 Parliamentary Elections, pp. 5-6; on Serbian 2012 Parliamentary and Early Presidential Elections, p. 22; on Georgian 2012 Parliamentary Elections, p. 7; on Moldovian 2011 Local Elections, p. 25.

[102] OSCE/ODIHR Final Election Observation Reports on Croatian 2011 Parliamentary Elections, p. 18; Election Assessment Reports on Slovenian 2011 Early Elections for the National Assembly p. 8; on Spanish 2011 Early Parliamentary Elections, p. 18; and on Estonian 2011 Parliamentary Elections, p. 23.

[103] OSCE/ODIHR Final Election Observation Report on Ukrainian 2012 Parliamentary Elections, p. 7.

[104] OSCE/ODIHR Final Election Observation Report on Croatian 2011 Parliamentary Elections, p. 17.

subject to certain restrictions, as set out in the relevant international treaties. However, the passive election right must be respected without discrimination. There is no genuine election without a plurality of genuine choices. Therefore, single-party dominance is contrary to the OSCE commitments.

Electoral Administration: Whereas no specific OSCE commitment exists with respect to electoral administration, from the OSCE commitments as a whole, it transpires that elections must be administered impartially and independently. The ODIHR election observation reports regularly assess the work of the election administration in terms of their inclusiveness, effectiveness and efficiency.[105] Consensual decision-making is one of the indicators that partisan interests did not prevail in the electoral administration.[106] The election bodies' work with respect to electoral disputes must be of the same quality as a decision made by an independent arbiter.

Electoral Campaign: Freedom of political association, of expression[107] and equal treatment of political groups must be ensured, i.e., no one should gain unlawful and unfair advantage by *inter alia* abusing state resources for its own campaigning. Free political campaigning and equal media access are a prerequisite for informed voters who only then can freely express their opinion. Elections must be free from any violence or pressure: states must ensure that all candidates freely carry out their campaigning and that political pluralism is protected.[108] Donations should be clearly regulated, with specific ceilings imposed.[109] State resources must be treated separately from the party resources and must not be abused in a campaign.

Media must be impartial and give access to all electoral candidates under non-discriminatory rules in terms of price and allocation of time. Similarly, election competitors must respect the rules on financing and media access, which in turn must be clear and foreseeable. Private media should not exceed the allocated agreed time.[110]

---

[105] On impartial and independent administration see more in the OSCE Existing Commitments for Democratic Elections in OSCE Participating States (2003) p. 14.
[106] OSCE/ODIHR Final Election Observation Report on Macedonian 2008 Early Parliamentary Elections, p. 6.
[107] OSCE/ODIHR Final Election Assessment Report on Turkish 2011 Parliamentary Elections, p. 18.
[108] OSCE/ODIHR Final Election Observation Report on Kazakhstani 2012 Early Parliamentary Elections, p. 27.
[109] OSCE/ODIHR Final Election Assessment Report on Slovak 2010 Parliamentary Elections, p. 11.
[110] OSCE/ODIHR Statement of Preliminary Findings and Conclusions on Macedonian 2013 Municipal Elections 2nd round, p. 2; OSCE/ODIHR Final Election Assessment Report on Slovak 2010 Parliamentary

III. European Regional Organizations Developing Standards in the Election Field

Effective Remedy: Legal protection of the electoral process is not only implied in the electoral commitments, but it is also an indispensable element of the OSCE human rights' protection architecture. Bearing that in mind, an effective remedy means: a) impartial and independent administrative bodies and judiciary; b) administrative and judicial procedures which are public and transparent; c) available appeals for all aspects of the electoral process; d) proceedings concluded within short deadlines in order not to delay the final electoral results; and e) decisions that are reasoned and publicly available. During the pre-election phase, adequate and effective remedies must be in place for the voters' registration, nomination of candidates and violations of the electoral campaign rules by the candidates, the submitters of candidates' lists and the media. The criminal-law remedies must be effective enough to end impunity in election-related cases.[111]

Disadvantaged groups: The OSCE commitments require greater inclusion of women in political life, both as candidates and as members of election bodies. Gender quotas should be used as a mechanism to achieve it.[112] As for national minorities, information about electoral processes must be available in their languages, as well as voter education programmes for those minorities prone to intimidation.[113]

Election Day

Voters: The secrecy of ballots is a safeguard of the active election right and of the integrity of elections. Proper identification of voters is indispensable for protecting the equality of votes. Polling stations and voting must be accessible to persons with special needs in line with the principle of universality. Detainees must be allowed to vote in accordance with a presumption of innocence. Intimidations or any kind of pressures on voters must be effectively prohibited and suppressed.[114] Family, group, proxy and multiple voting is strictly interdicted. If e-voting is foreseen, it must be transparent and its integrity must be safeguarded.[115]

Elections, p. 14; OSCE Handbook on Media Monitoring for Election Observation Missions (2012) pp 13-14, 25-29; Final Election Observation Report on Croatian 2011 Parliamentary Elections, p. 18.
[111] Petit, ODIHR, Resolving Election Disputes in the OSCE Area: Towards A Standard Election Disputes Monitoring System (2000) pp. 6, 9-15 at <http:/www.osce.org>.
[112] Final Election Observation Report on Spanish 2011 Early Parliamentary Elections, p. 19; Final Election Observation Report on 2011 Parliamentary Elections in Turkey, p. 23.
[113] Final Election Observation Report on Slovak 2010 Parliamentary Elections, pp. 16-17.
[114] OSCE/ODIHR Final Election Observation Reports on 2012 Montenegrin Early Parliamentary Elections, p. 11; Final Election Assessment Reports on Spanish 2011 Early Parliamentary Elections, p. 21; on Turkish 2011

Counting: Counting of the votes must be done transparently and honestly, with official results made public for each polling station.

Security: All electoral participants, not only voters, must feel safe and secure. Any heavy unnecessary presence of the police might be intimidating not only for voters, candidates and their supporters, but also for the election administration. Therefore, effective and efficient prosecution and conviction of those held responsible for electoral offences is a necessary precondition for holding free and fair elections.

Post-election phase

Campaign Financing: The accountability of the electoral contestants is intrinsically linked with election expenditures reporting and auditing. Impartial and effective media monitoring and reporting is one of the safeguards against unlawful or excessive electoral campaign expenditure.[116]

Effective Resolution of Electoral Disputes: Post-election complaints and appeals must be dealt with in a timely manner, to enable the results to be published as soon as possible. Delayed results might raise suspicion regarding their accuracy. It follows that transparency and publicity at the level of administrative bodies and the courts are a, *sine qua non,* for effective resolution of electoral disputes.[117] There must be an effective remedy to challenge election results. Election results that have been tampered with must be invalidated, regardless of their impact on the electoral outcome. Otherwise, the voters whose votes were annulled could not contribute to the election of their representatives. This is also important in case of public funding received per vote gained.

Mandate Entrusted to a Winning Candidate: An honest tabulation and public reporting of the electoral outcome must result in the elected office being taken by a candidate chosen in line

---

Parliamentary Elections, p. 25; on Slovak 2010 Parliamentary Elections, p. 19; on UK 2005 General Elections, p. 14.
[115] OSCE/ODIHR Supplementary Human Dimension Meeting "Challenges of Election Technologies and Procedures", Final Report (2005) pp. 3-4; OSCE/ODIHR 2008 Discussion Paper in preparation of Guidelines for the Observation of Electronic Voting at<http:/www.osce.org>.
[116] OSCE/ODIHR Final Election Assessment Reports on Finnish 2011 Parliamentary Elections, pp.13-14; and on Slovak 2010 Parliamentary Elections, pp. 10-11, 13.
[117] OSCE/ODIHR Final Election Assessment Report on Turkish 2011 Parliamentary Elections, p. 21.

with the electoral formula foreseen by law. The winning candidates must be installed and occupy the office until expiration of their term.

2.2. Detecting Challenges Related to the OSCE Electoral Commitments

The last century concluded with a challenge to democratize the former socialist countries. The new century began with the challenge to deepen democracy. The detected electoral challenges for OSCE participating states focus on two questions: -the first one relates to the conceptualization of the OSCE election standards,[118] and the second one to their implementation, or rather to the lack of their proper implementation.

Relating to the first area of concern, the very existence of the OSCE electoral commitments was challenged, or alternatively they were not considered detailed enough by certain participating states. Russia and the CIS countries engaged in the debate about the supplementary election commitments, the so-called "Copenhagen Plus",[119] by stating that the OSCE election commitments did not adequately address the protection of vulnerable groups. Plus they were in their opinion only vague and non-binding standards subject to individual interpretation.[120] The idea of OSCE legally-binding election commitments was rejected, but the drafting of additional commitments, especially in view of new voting technologies and regarding the election rights of vulnerable groups, was considered.[121] Nevertheless, so far no supplementary electoral commitments were adopted.

The question is raised as to whether or not the possibility of introduce supplementary commitments was at that time seen as a way to resolve the difficulties that arose between ODIHR and some participating states, linked to ODIHR's reporting of a non-observance of the OSCE electoral commitments. An additional reason might be to avoid further objections about the lack of precision of the standing commitments, which does not allow a proper

---

[118] The Report from the 2012 Supplementary Human Dimension Meeting, Session I.
[119] The 2002 Porto Document and Ministerial Decision no. 5/2003.
[120] The CIS countries, which are also OSCE countries, started observing elections since 2002-2003. There was a difference in the opinion between the ODIHR and the CIS observers as to how much the observed elections complied with the election standards.
[121] Ghebali, Debating Election and Election Monitoring Standards at the OSCE: Between Technical Needs and Politicization, OSCE Yearbook (2006) pp. 218-221.

electoral assessment. The ODIHR Note on the Supplementary Commitments seems to confirm this, as it states that the record of implementation of the Copenhagen Document and post-Copenhagen declarations and decisions to-date, would indicate that the discussion on additional commitments on democratic elections to supplement the existing ones was appropriate. However, since no new commitments have been agreed upon, this clearly indicates that difficulty exists in the decision-making and consensus of the participating states in this regard. The problem that Russian Federation had with electoral commitments did not lay in the commitments as such, but in their interpretation.[122]

If there is political will, the OSCE electoral commitments may grow into being more comprehensive and precise, even if their legal form does not change. It is worthwhile to mention the difference made between the original and interpretative standards: the first ones relate to the commitments set out in the OSCE documents, while the second ones relate to the specific standards on which ODIHR bases its election assessments. Whereas the original standards contain principles that reflect the states' obligations assumed by other international instruments (UDHR, ICCPR, ECHR) they are not so precise and comprehensive with respect to the standards relating to different topics of elections. In particular, electoral campaign financing (public and private funding) has not been tackled at all, while the obligations to regulate private and public media for the purposes of electoral campaign remain a vague obligation for the states.[123] For the latter, it is desirable to clarify the type of the media access to which the electoral competitors are entitled (proportional or strict equality).[124] Regarding the participation of women, there are existing obligations, but they are placed in a gender related documents, such as the OSCE Action Plan for Promoting Gender Equality. Since the under-representation of women in political sphere remains a problem, it is desirable to include more precise "original" election-related commitments to promote the equality between genders. The same goes for an impartial electoral administration and the resolution of electoral disputes mentioned above, as supplementary, but vital commitments to ensure "free and fair elections" in the OSCE region.

---

[122] Evers, OSCE Election Observation (2010) at <http ://www.core-hamburg.de>.
[123] OSCE/ODIHR, OSCE Human Dimension Commitments, 1 Thematic Compilation 3rd edition (2011) pp. 123-125 at <http:/www.osce.org>.
[124] OSCE/ODIHR Final Election Observation Report on Croatian 2011 Parliamentary Elections, p. 18.

The interpretative standards derived from the original commitments are much more comprehensive, precise and clear. In view of ODIHR's methodology, and according to ODIHR's election observation reports, it appears that the election standards have been applied consistently and coherently. Still, it is the interpretation and application of those standards by ODIHR which has been challenged by certain participating states.[125]

Including the standard of meaningful representation in the OSCE original commitments will guide governments to deepen democracy, especially in the plural societies of the OSCE region. As a standard of electoral outcome, meaningful representation belongs to the post-election period. However, it entails conceptualization of an electoral system that will allow political representation of all segments of society in the political decision-making. There is a synergy between meaningful representation and the universality and equality of the vote, and it can be defined as its by-product. Judging by the "electoral inclusiveness trend", meaningful representation is becoming the essence of contemporary democracies. It not only provides a protective umbrella for marginalized groups in society, but it also defends the democratic system of governance by protecting participation in public affairs by the opposition, and asking for true accountability of the government to the representatives of the people. Furthermore, if political decisions are taken by the majority, the minorities must be protected. In absence of legal guarantees for minorities, they will be left to the mercy of the majority.[126]

Elections are not a goal in and of themselves, but rather, they are a method for installing, nurturing and protecting democracy. Then, what should be done when forces promoting intolerance rise to power by elections, or the opposition is wiped out in an election, or it exists only on ethnic or religious divisions? While there are practical arrangements in place for enhancement of the participation of voters, minorities and women, there is no clear method how to ensure that the minority political interests assume a meaningful place in democracy.[127] Inclusion of a standard of meaningful representation in the OSCE commitments will assist that goal.

---

[125] Evers, OSCE Election Observation (2010) at <http ://www.core-hamburg.de>, pp. 245-250. On low turnout of voters as a sign of political inequality, see Lijphart, Patterns of Democracy (Serbian translation, published by Sluzbeni List SCG Beograd) (1999) p. 271.

[126] Lijphart, Patterns of Democracy (Serbian translation, published by Sluzbeni List CG Beograd) (1999) pp. 22-23, 33, 37, 48-49, 58-59, 75-78, 171, 340.

[127] About the majority democracy as a system excluding the opposition from a decision-making, ibid pp. 95-96.

Proper implementation of the OSCE commitments, relates to the second issue of concern. It goes hand in hand with the discussion about the principles and methodology on which the ODIHR based its election observations, as the electoral watchdog.

The "proper implementation problem" of electoral commitments has three aspects. The first one relates to the lack of observance of the OSCE commitments by the participating states, as documented by the ODIHR election observation reports.

The second one is closely related to election observation as conducted by ODIHR. This OSCE institution has been both admired and criticised for its election observation activities. It appears that the criticism of ODIHR's work started when serious flaws during certain countries' elections were recorded by the respective EOMs.[128] Furthermore, in 2009, the ODIHR has struggled to receive states' invitations to observe elections, which is a pre-condition for election observation. However, looking at the other side of a coin, in order not to endorse rigged elections, the OSCE/ODIHR may also refuse to send election observation missions.[129] The reasons for the refusal are to be found in the existence of conditions under which it is impossible to hold free and fair elections, like the existence of oligarchy and participation of military and persons involved in war crimes in the government (Tajikistan). Limitation of the election observation mission in terms of time frame, the composition of the mission and the granting of visas to the observation team were considered obstacles to sending an ODIHR observation mission (Russian Federation).

The last facet of the "proper implementation problem" underscores the need for a systematic follow-up of the ODIHR observation recommendations. In cases of persistent election violations, despite OSCE/ODIHR election assistance, there must be a well-defined and transparent course of action for the OSCE and its participating States.[130] Such course of action must go beyond public statements and rejection to observe elections. The OSCE participating states must have the power to impose a penalty on the violator of the electoral commitments, amounting to terminating the cooperation and communication with such governments.

---

[128] OSCE/ODIHR, Common Responsibility Commitments and Implementation (2006) pp. 34-35 at <http:/www.osce.org.
[129] Kelly, Monitoring Democracy (2013) pp. 47-48, 59.
[130] On denial of the legitimacy of elections due to electoral irregularities, see Kelly, Monitoring Democracy (2013) pp. 174-175.

III. European Regional Organizations Developing Standards in the Election Field

To conclude, the OSCE commitments are as alive and important today, as they were on the day when they were agreed upon for the development of genuine democracy. Although they are not legally-binding they still equally apply to all of the OSCE participating states. The original and interpretative commitments have become a norm, a standard that tailors "free and fair elections" in the OSCE region.

In light of some of the participating states' persistent failure to observe the relevant OSCE commitments, it is clear that systematic, complete and more effective follow-up is lacking. With respect to the on-going debate within the OSCE about the reform of the monitoring mechanisms in order to overcome the detected weaknesses, it is clear that it must also foresee effective remedies to deter any continued violations of the OSCE commitments, while preserving the impartiality and neutrality of the mechanism. It should also try to avoid duplications of efforts and incongruity not only with other international and regional organizations, but also between various OSCE bodies.

3. European Union

The EU was inspired by representative democracy since its inception. In the EU Treaty and the Treaty of Amsterdam, democracy and respect for human rights as guaranteed by the ECHR were mentioned as fundamental values of the EU order.[131] Moreover, the Preamble of the Charter of the Fundamental Rights of the EU (the Charter) reiterates the commitment to the principles of democracy, featuring it as one of the pillars of the Union. However, it does not contain any other element of citizen participation in public life, with the exception of elections for the EP and local self-government units. The right to good administration cannot be considered sufficient to fill the lacuna in the Charter[132], in the sense of citizen inclusiveness element.[133]

In order to underpin democracy, the 2009 ToL contains elaborated provisions for establishing a closer link between the EU institutions and citizens. It attempts to meet the concern about the citizen participation[134] by reinforcing the EU internal democracy. While reiterating democracy as a sole political system of governance[135], the ToL confers greater powers upon the EP, foresees greater involvement by citizens in European affairs, and aims at increased accountability to the citizens. Nonetheless, the ToL did not rebut entirely the "democratic deficit" criticism, *inter alia,* due to the lack of political contestation at the EU level. In this context, it is also questionable how the European Council and the Council of the EU can answer for EU policies at a pan-European level, when the officials can only be held accountable at the national level. Furthermore, the EU member states have not yet transferred real power to the directly elected EP in some areas, such as enlargement. As a result, the EP's influence over certain Council decisions is reduced to approval, discussion and consultation.

Despite the "democracy deficit" criticism, the EU plays an important role in the democratization of the ex-socialist countries, through its enlargement process. The applicable

---

[131] Jacobs, White, Ovey, The European Convention on Human Rights (4th edition) (2004) p. 516.
[132] Article 41 of the Charter.
[133] Dahl, What Large Scale Democracy Needs? Political Science Quarterly vol. 120, no. 2 (2005) pp. 188-189, 197.
[134] Bogdanor, Legitimacy, Accountability and Democracy in the European Union, A Federal Trust Report (2007).
[135] Articles 1A and 10A (on external action) of the ToL.

1993 Copenhagen Criteria[136] require free, fair and multiparty elections, the stability of democratic institutions, a separation of powers, good governance and protection of human rights and of the rights of minorities. For a candidate country to be successful in its aspirations, it is necessary that these criteria are observed in practice. The criteria have been criticized for their broadness and over inclusiveness, which in turn causes difficulties for their objective assessment and may result in a double measuring stick for the candidate countries (especially regarding the protection of the rights of minorities).[137] EU enlargement has been and still is an important instrument, between stick and carrot for the promotion of effective observance of democratic principles among the candidate countries. However, in some cases, observance of the above criteria is not the only basis for measuring the progress of a country towards the EU. Some EU countries, in order to push their own agendas, use the enlargement process, which may be counterproductive in terms of observation of democratic principles as a pre-condition for stability and security of the European continent. Such a situation is counterproductive from the point of view of democratic consolidation, as the national parliaments of the candidate countries must adopt the *acquis* as they stand. If the country has a real prospect of a membership, the lack of participation in the creation of the *acquis* can be corrected once it becomes a full EU member. However, the problem arises when a country does not have a realistic timely perspective for the EU membership, and yet undertakes a costly and lengthy transposition of the EU *acquis* into its legislation, without the real participation from its elected representatives and with no public consultations. The concern raised should not be ignored, since EU enlargement is an important instrument to support democracy taking a permanent hold on the European continent, thus contributing towards its stability and security.[138]

3.1. Electoral Democracy in the EU

In spite of Article 8A, paragraph 1 of the ToL, which stipulate that the EU is based on representative democracy, the electoral opportunity remains extended only with respect to the

---

[136] Accetto, United in Crisis: The Development of the European Union through Concrete Problems (2009) pp. 4-6.

[137] Kochenov, Behind the Copenhagen Facade. The meaning and Structure of the Copenhagen Political Criterion of Democracy and the Rule of Law, European Integration Online Papers vol. 8 (2004).

[138] Levitsky, Way, Autocracy by Democratic Rules: The Dynamics of Competitive Authoritarianism in the Post Cold War Era (rev. 2003) pp. 3 and 10.

election of the EP,[139] although a number of top EU offices are vested with "pan-European" competencies. If the trend of deepening of relations between the EU countries continues, citizens should be vested with greater election powers in the future. In view of the important functions and tasks executed by the European Commission, it appears that the EU citizens will be very much interested in participating in direct elections of the president of the European Commission, for the following reasons:

First, the current election and appointment systems of top officials in the EU do not lead to a result where the whole of the EU is represented by a "personnage" elected by all European citizens. Direct elections of the president of the European Commission will bring EU policies closer to EU citizens, thus resulting in greater political involvement of the electors. Second, such an election will represent a counter argument to the "democracy deficit" discourse, as EU citizens will hold the president of the European Commission directly accountable. Third, it will require greater education and information on the part of the electorate, and thus it will refresh the interest of citizens in EU issues. Fourth, the candidates running for this office will have to devote much more time and energy to pan-European issues, in order to attract votes from all parts of the EU. Finally, voters do not need delegate the election of the president of the European Commission to their directly elected representatives, when they can do this job better, and with greater benefits for European integration. Any objections raised in this regard that such a system may only result in the electoral victory of candidates coming from bigger and more powerful countries may be rebutted by a nomination system based on the principles of equality, non-discrimination and fairness.

Now, turning to the EP, which has been directly elected since 1979. The EP elections, which are held at 5-year intervals, are rather perceived as being 28 separate elections[140] and different from national elections,[141] albeit EU citizens directly elect their representatives in this institution. Legal reasons, among others, for the above conclusion stem from the manner of the EP election, with the applicable provisions scattered in a number of documents. According to the Preamble of the 2002 amended Act concerning the election of the

---

[139] Gallagher, Laver, Mair, Representative Government in Modern Europe (fifth edition) (2011) pp. 155-157.
[140] OSCE/ODIHR, Elections to the European Parliament 4 - 7 June 2009, Expert Group Report 11 – 30 May 2009, pp. 1 and 11.
[141] Gallagher, Laver, Mair, Representative Government in Modern Europe (fifth edition) (2011) p. 127.

representatives of the EP by direct universal suffrage, there are three legal pillars on which the EP elections are based:

The primary pillar for the EP elections is composed of the EU primary and secondary legislation.[142] In line with the universal vote principle, ToL has reaffirmed the Charter's individual approach in granting passive and active election rights to EU citizens for the EP and municipal elections, based on the place of their residence at the time of elections. The states are under an obligation to grant equivalent election rights to their EU co-patriot non-nationals. Thus, the principles of equality and non-discrimination underlined throughout the text of the ToL and the Charter also apply to electoral affairs. The dynamism of the EU and of the rights to political association and the passive election right create an impetus for comprehensive electoral reform envisaged by Article 190 of the Treaty on the Functioning of the EU as amended by the ToL. Similar to the Charter, the revisions introduced by the ToL contain minimalist language with respect to the EU electoral rules. The EP elections must be direct in compliance with "free and fair elections" principles. Electoral rights may be subject to limitations grounded in law. However, the EU general principle of proportionality applies in this regard. A restriction must match the aim sought, it must be necessary and it must not impose too heavy a burden on an individual. Along with the protection of the rights of others, the Charter foresees another broadly-worded admissible aim for restriction of rights: general interest recognized by the EU.

More meat on the bones, figuratively speaking, is found in the secondary sources of EU law. The electoral systems, the equality of the vote, the incompatibility of functions and dispute resolution under the EU legal framework are the intersection points that cut across national

---

[142] The EU pieces of legislation governing the EP elections are as follows: ToL- Article 9A3, amended Articles 17, paragraph 2b and 19 of Treaty on Functioning of EU; 190, paragraph 1 (EP) of ToL; Charter- Articles 39 and 52 of the Charter; Act concerning the election of the members of the European Parliament by direct universal suffrage, annexed to Council Decision 76/787/ECSC, EEC, Euratom, Official Journal, OJ L 278, dated 8 October 1976, p. 1 amended by Council Decision 2002/772/EC, Euratom, Official Journal OJ L 283, dated 21 January 2002, p. 1; Regulation (EC) No 2004/2003 of the European Parliament and of the Council dated 4 November 2003 on the regulations governing political parties at European level and the rules regarding their funding, Official Journal L 297, dated 15 November 2003, p. 1; Directive 93/109/EC laying down detailed arrangements for the exercise of the right to vote and stand as a candidate in elections to the European Parliament for citizens of the Union residing in a Member State of which they are not nationals, Official Journal L 329, dated 30 December 1993, p. 34; Commission Recommendation dated 12 March 2013 on enhancing the democratic and efficient conduct of the elections to the European Parliament 2013/142/EU, Official Journal L 79/29 dated 21 March 2013. The 2003 Accession Act also contains applicable provisions.

boundaries. On the electoral system: - EU member states are not free to opt for the majoritarian electoral system, regardless of their traditions, but can choose variations of the proportional electoral model. Thresholds may not exceed 5%. On the equality of votes: - it is safeguarded by giving to all EU citizens the right to vote only once, and by requiring constituencies that reflect the proportional nature of the election. On the incompatibility of functions: -accumulation with high EU and/or national offices (e.g. a member of national parliament) is proscribed in order to avoid a conflict of interest, as well as double payments from public funds. On disputes: -only disputes centered around the EU legal framework are dealt with by the EP.

The Act does not elaborate much on electoral campaign financing, as it only gives the right to the states to impose a ceiling on electoral campaign financing, or to refrain from it. The European political parties' funding is regulated in greater detail.[143]

Because the EP election day is not a single-day event throughout the EU, there is a requirement to make public the results only after the last of the countries has concluded its election, in order not to influence another country's election.

Last but not least, municipal elections in the member states are also regulated[144] by way of secondary legislation not in terms of "free and fair" electoral criteria, but as practical arrangements giving equal electoral rights to EU citizens, albeit non-nationals. Municipal elections do not cover national elections or elections of a regional legislature, and derogations are possible under certain general conditions. In view of the Charter of Local Self Government's list of ratifications, it follows that its "free and fair" election standards apply to EU countries' municipal elections.

The second pillar embodies the electoral principles common to all member states. In this regard, the 2009 ToL[145] referring to European elections speaks about "common principles" as an alternative to "a uniform procedure in all Member States". Since the EU member states seem far from reaching an agreement on an entirely uniform electoral procedure, the common electoral principles should continue safeguarding the equality of treatment across EU state

---

[143] Regulation (EC) no. 2004/2003 of the European Parliament and of the Council dated 4 November 2003 on the regulations governing political parties at European level and the rules regarding their funding, as amended by Regulation (EC) no. 1524/2007, dated 27 December 2007.
[144] Directive 94/80/EC on the right to vote and stand as a candidate in municipal elections dated 20 January 1995, amended by the Council Directive 96/30/EC dated 13 May 1996.
[145] Article 190, paragraph 1.

boundaries. In addition to EU legislation, the ECHR Protocol 1-3 also contains common principles that should be applicable in the EU, because of the following arguments: a) both the EU Charter and the ToL reaffirm the fundamental value of the ECHR in the human rights arena; b) each EU member is a party to the ECHR Protocol 1, Article 3; and c) the EP elections fall within the ambit of this article. Another argument, albeit not so strong legally speaking, can be made about the OSCE commitments' inclusion in the "common principles". They are approved by all EU members, and serve as a guide for enlightened understanding of "free and fair elections" in the EU region.

On a broader level of principles, the general principles of the EU, like respect for fundamental rights, equality and proportionality, which are tackled below, should not be left out of the electoral sources' catalogue. With respect to electoral legislation, the general EU principles of legal certainty and legitimate expectation are also applicable in the EU and in its member states. The observance of the general principle of transparency is indispensable for elections as a safeguard of their integrity.

Indeed, the ECJ, through its case-law, has reminded the member states that general principles of EU law like equal treatment, prevention of discrimination and respect for human rights are alive and kicking also in the electoral area. Even more interesting is the ECJ's conclusion that a lack of general principle in the electoral franchise segment allows member state to freely regulate it.[146] What is surprising about this judgment is the ECJ's referral to the electoral principles of secret, direct, universal and free (mentioned-above), without listing equal suffrage as a key electoral principle. The ECJ omitted the principle of equal suffrage although it belongs to the European electoral heritage. Does this mean that controversy about the "digressive proportionality" in the EP[147] contributes to the pragmatic interpretation of the key electoral principles? The counter-argument is rooted in the *sui generis* nature of the EU and of the EP; and in the EU's deepening pace. Yet the principle of equal suffrage should not be forgotten in the EU architecture of democracy. Even more so, given that it could be hypothetically challenged before the ECtHR.

---

[146] Spain v. United Kingdom, ECJ (Grand Chamber), C-145-04, 12 September 2006, para 33.
[147] Gallagher, Laver, Mair, Representative Government in Modern Europe (fifth edition) (2011) pp. 125-126.

The third pillar is the national electoral legislation of each EU state, which regulates European elections, as well as municipal elections. Since the EU electoral rules are requisite for the EP and municipal elections, the EU requires a transposition of the pieces of electoral legislation. For example, the proportional electoral system foreseen in the EU rules, has an impact on the composition of the EP, as it allows for a wider representation of various parties and segments of the society when compared with the majority system.[148] The imposition of an upper limit on the electoral threshold goes along the same lines. Freedom of movement and establishment within the EU goes hand in hand with granting election rights to non-nationals. In turn, it requires cooperation among the EU member states in order to compile and maintain accurate voters' lists of the EU member states.

On-going electoral reform in the EU attempts to deepen and harmonize electoral democracy and accommodate the needs of all 28 EU member states. For example, the EP elections should be held on a common day throughout Europe and political parties should disclose their alliance at the European level on the ballot, as well as their preferred candidate for the European Commission president. A motion is filed with the effect to terminate the EU funding of the rightist parties that promote intolerance and racisms.

3.2. Applicable Election Standards in the EU – Electoral Cycle Approach

The following specific vertical and horizontal election requirements can be discerned in respect of the EU electoral competition:

Pre-election phase

Electoral system and law: Different variations of the proportional representation model are acceptable (closed lists, single transferrable vote, preferential vote). The electoral threshold is also a subject of the predilection of the member state, but must not exceed 5%.

Voters: All EU adult citizens have the right directly to elect their representatives in the EP in accordance with the universality principle. National legislation governs the eligibility of the

---

[148] Gallagher, Laver, Mair, Representative Government in Modern Europe (fifth edition) (2011) pp. 398-399.

voters. However, under no circumstances (e.g. current residence) may states discriminate against EU citizens who are not their nationals. An objective justification, or conditions for derogation (e.g., in case of Luxemburg, where non-nationals exceed 20%) constitute exception to this rule. Active registration for non-nationals is acceptable, who must be informed about the elections. EU countries are under an obligation to exchange information regarding their voters in order to disable double voting in two different states, and to ensure accurate voters' lists.

Candidates: The principle of equality and non-discrimination applies also with respect to the nomination of candidates, governed by national legislations of the 28 countries, as well as for the candidates proposed by the European parties. Regardless of the principles of non-discrimination and equality, individual candidates are not given the right to stand for EP elections in each of the EU member states. In addition, an equitable gender representation is nowhere explicitly foreseen in the EU electoral rules, although equal rights are guaranteed by the Charter. Dual mandate is prohibited, as well as accumulation of top offices, both at national and EU levels.

Electoral campaign: The electoral campaign financing rules foresee a ceiling of EUR 12,000 per year and per donor for the European parties. The parties must observe a transparency requirement in terms of annual disclosure of their financial reports and of the source of donations exceeding 500 euro. They must refuse anonymous donations, with the aim of ensuring transparent and responsible spending of EU public funds. The obligation for annual disclosure of funds disbursed to the parties also extends to the EP. Sources of funding declared inadmissible in order to avoid a conflict of interest and undue interference comprise donations from the budgets of the EP political groups, from any company under influence of a public authority, or from non-EU countries. The admissible sources of funding comprise contributions from national political parties (members of a political party at the European level) and from national political foundations (members of a political foundation at the European level), provided that they do not exceed 40% of the annual budget of the political party or foundation at the European level.

Legal remedies: They must be available regarding active and passive election rights to non-nationals under the same principles of equality and non-discrimination. The transparency principle also applies in this regard.

Election Day

Voting procedure: The EP voting takes place in a 4-day span of time, as EU citizens vote on different days for the EP.

Post-election phase

Election results: No publication of electoral results is allowed until the last election is concluded, in order to avoid any influence on the voters.

Electoral Disputes: The EP has competence to deal with electoral disputes connected with EU legislation in a transparent procedure. The ECJ also has competence to adjudicate electoral disputes relating to active and passive election rights.

The above-established specific election standards show that large portions of different elements of the electoral cycle remain governed by national legislation. As a result of the inter-state political negotiations, the EU election standards build on the already existing election standards in Europe, but also on the electoral legislation of each state. From the plans for electoral reform, it transpires that new election standards are not a priority. It does not appear that unified electoral legislation will represent a sole remedy for the electoral problems detected in different countries (e.g., the impossibility to stand for election as individual candidate, a lack of judicial remedy, a dissonance in the criteria attached to the exercise of the election rights). The same effects can be achieved by way of progressive approximation of the respective national legislation.

Looking at the effects of the ECJ's aforementioned judgments that were passed 7 years ago, it appears as though the EU feels uninspired to fill-in the electoral lacunas. Indeed, the approximation of the electoral legislation even for the EP elections, keeps taking baby steps. The reasons why the member states would not feel an urgent need for a greater coherence in the electoral field, may originate from its impact on the election results, and their fear of a change affecting their national political balance. Certain member states are slow in loosening their grip on electoral rules, although they are under an obligation to transpose the EU electoral law in their national legislation under the same rules valid for other common fields.

Whereas there are no EU laws governing general or presidential elections, they should not suffer from lowering the election standards in comparison to the EP elections. For instance, the financial campaign rules valid for the EP elections should, by analogy, apply to other types of elections in the EU member states. The above-mentioned general principles of the EU also feed into national electoral rules for all types of elections. Common electoral principles, as framed by the European constitutional and electoral heritage, represent yet another facet of the generally applicable electoral rules. However, the electoral systems for the country level elections remain an undefined variable. Specific rules and measures about how to implement the common electoral principles are also sketched by the countries, with a caveat that they are still bound by the CoE and the OSCE specific or interpretative election standards.

In this context, introducing the standard of a meaningful representation as a reflection of broader inclusiveness, could address the low turnout of the voters in all 28 countries by strengthening the link between the grassroots and supranational levels. It will also enhance the representation of women and minorities in the EP by clearly setting out such a requirement in EU legislation. Still, it appears that for the time being any attempt to substantially enhance EU electoral rules is doomed to fail.

4. Harmonization of European Election Standards: Outlook for the Future

The practice of electoral democracy inextricably links various sets of standards derived from the European instruments. The current situation of many different sets of electoral general and specific standards does not bring clarity in their country-by-country application. The turmoil in the normative sphere has been reflected in the practical dimension of "free and fair" elections, as it follows from the OSCE/ODIHR election observation reports in the European region. The turmoil is not related to the main electoral principles, i.e., free, fair, regular, universal, equal, direct. On the contrary, there is a high level of harmonization in this regard. The confusion appears when those principles are translated into concrete and specific standards for each electoral topic.

Based on the results of the examination and on the conclusions, the following proposition is made for the outlook of the paradigm of "free and fair elections" in Europe. It is based on the principles of universal, fair, equal, regular, direct and genuine elections, as follows:

Pre-election phase

Electoral system and law

The electoral model reflects the principles of the paradigm of "free and fair" for all types of elections (legislative, presidential, municipal, regional, mayoral). Whereas the countries' electoral systems are shaped in accordance with their traditions and needs, they incorporate the following:

-Periodic direct elections ensure that the elected collective body reflects the will of the electors. The mandate should not exceed 5 years.

-A requirement for a meaningful representation ensures that disadvantaged groups are not impeded in the exercise of their election rights by, e.g., high thresholds. It further demands a proactive approach from the state in ensuring meaningful representation of women and minorities (e.g., by quotas, targets or reserved seats). A meaningful representation standard requires a plurality of electoral choices for the voters, and a type of electoral system that allows the widest possible representation of all segments of society in decision-making.

The electoral legislation is adopted and amended in line with democratic law-making, meaning that:

-There is an on-going dialogue with the ruling parties, the opposition and the disadvantaged groups. They are consulted, their views are taken into consideration and reasons are given when their comments are not accepted.

-The law is last amended at least a year before elections, in order to provide the conditions for a well-organized and successful election.

-The electoral legislation, which is based on the principles of equality before law, non-discrimination and inclusiveness is clear, coherent and accessible. Retroactive application of electoral legislation is prohibited.

III. European Regional Organizations Developing Standards in the Election Field

Voters

They have the following rights:

-To be well informed about all electoral options, including the parties, candidates, and about the political programmes offered.

-To be educated about the meaning of the election and, the ramifications in case they do not go out to vote, as well as about the voting procedures.

-To enjoy the right to a universal vote and to be included in the voters' list, when they are eligible. Permissible exceptions are: age, a lack of nationality, mental impairment (individually assessed), non-residence, conviction and imprisonment for serious or election-related crimes, but not for longer than necessary.

-To have an effective remedy regarding voter registration, not only for themselves, but also to challenge improper enfranchisement of others.

-To nominate their candidates as a group of citizens.

The States have the following obligations vis-a-vis the voters:

-To enfranchise every citizen who qualifies as a voter.

-To prepare and maintain accurate and up-to-date voters' list by introducing effective ways of registration and deletion of the persons who no longer qualify as voters from the voters' list.

-To protect personal data from the voters' list.

-To define the constituencies in line with the principle of the equality of votes, with a deviation not exceeding 10%. The delimitation should result in electoral districts of a similar size that are regularly re-adjusted, in view of the population change. The constituencies should respect ethnic, natural and geographical specificities. Gerrymandering is prohibited.

Candidates

They have the following rights:

-To be registered as candidates when they fulfill the legal requirements. Permissible restrictions relate to age, incompatibility of offices (the accumulation of elected offices, accumulation of executive, judicial, legislative and civil servants offices), mental impairments (individually assessed), a lack of residence or of citizenship, reimbursable and not excessive electoral deposit.

-To be treated equally before the law in line with the non-discrimination principle, regardless of who nominates them, i.e., the ruling party, the opposition, or if they are individual candidates.

-To be able to reach out to the voters through the media and to organize rallies. To organize the electoral campaign under the terms that will ensure the equality of chances of winning the election.

The states have the following obligations vis-à-vis the candidates:

-To ensure transparency in the nomination and approval process.

-To protect candidates from intimidation, threats, coercion and violence, and to restrain from interfering with their electoral campaign and private life.

-To ensure freedom of expression, of association, of peaceful assembly, of movement, and the right to privacy.

-To ensure funding and other advantages with the aim of facilitating electoral campaigning under equitable and fair conditions.

Electoral campaign

The electoral campaign financing rules foresee the following:

-All types of corruption (active and passive) and conflicts of interest (including ownership or a position which entails decision-making power over the media) are prohibited.

-There is a separation between the state and the parties.

-There is an explicit limit on donations, with a lower limit for donations made by individuals. Multinational corporations, including those registered in the country, cannot make donations.

-Anonymous and foreign donations are prohibited.

-Donations cannot be made by the state, regional or municipal bodies, enterprises or companies that have contracts with those bodies or which are under their influence. No administrative resources can be used for the purpose of election campaigning.

-Public funds are disbursed to candidates under the principles of equity, non-discrimination and proportionality. Party fees can also be used for the electoral campaign.

-There is a limit to the electoral expenditure. No expenditures are allowed outside of the organized electoral campaign.

-Inflow of cash and expenditure passes through an election agent and an election account for each organizer of the electoral campaign.

-The organizers of the electoral campaign must thoroughly record all financial details relating to elections. They must report their inflow and expenditures before, during and after the electoral campaign ends in line with the transparency requirement. They must also report all electoral campaign expenditures that were conducted in favor of their candidate by an entity/individual other than the electoral campaign organizer. A standardized financial report includes the source and the type of the source of funding (in-kind, monetary or other kind of advantage, donation, fees, loans, public subsidies), a description, the amount/value, venue and time of the activities, type and amount of the expenditure.

-The public is provided with information regarding electoral campaign financing, no later than 6 months from the day the electoral campaign ended.

-All organizers of the electoral campaign are audited by an independent auditor.

-Adequate monitoring of electoral expenses is in place.

-Legal remedy is in place for a breach of the applicable rules.

The media are regulated as follows:

-Private and public media, print and electronic media are impartial and fair when reporting about electoral candidates' campaign. There is no government or other unwarranted interference with the media.

-Free time is allocated by electronic public and private media under equitable and fair conditions.

-For paid electoral campaign activities, the media must not give unfair advantages by giving higher discounts, or not requesting a payment for their services. It must always be denoted who ordered the paid advertisement or a public survey poll.

-Paid advertisements are accessible under equitable and non-discriminatory rules in terms of price and allocation of time. The media do not exceed the allocated time per candidate.

-There is an independent and impartial body that regulates and monitors electronic and print media.

Legal remedies

They are available to safeguard all aspects of the pre-electoral phase:

-Administrative and criminal law remedies effectively protect active and passive election rights.

-Respect for the media rules and electoral campaign financing is ensured, without undue interferences.

-The division of competencies between prosecutors, administrative bodies and the courts is clearly defined. Guarantees are in place for their independence and impartiality.

-Judicial and administrative procedures are transparent, public and efficient in view of the specific nature of elections. They are completed without causing undue delays to the declaration of the electoral results.

-Decisions are amenable to judicial review.

-Effective sanctions are in place to deter illegal behavior and suppress electoral impunity.

-No amnesty is granted to the offenders convicted of election-related offences.

Election observation

In line with the existing commitments, international and local election observers are:

-Allowed to observe elections in all their stages including counting and tallying of the votes, and protected against any attempts of coercion or threats.

-Provided with full access to polling stations, to the electoral management bodies and to court sessions.

-Provided with access to documents, including minutes from the counting and tallying, appeals, decisions and judgments.

Electoral Administration

Elections are administered impartially and independently, meaning that:

-All levels of the electoral administration are composed in a way which ensures the impartiality and independence of their decision-making. The highest electoral bodies are professional, permanent and have sufficient resources to complete their task.

-Members of the electoral bodies are safe from threats, pressures and violence.

-Decision-making is timely, effective and open to public scrutiny.

-Decisions of the electoral bodies are public.

-Integrity of the electoral process is ensured in all phases, starting from the protection of the electoral material to imposition of fines in case of violations of electoral rules.

-Voters are educated about elections in the languages they understand.

<u>Election Day</u>

Voters

They have the following rights:

-To cast a secret vote free from coercion, threats, violence or manipulations.

-To obtain voting instructions, information about the candidates and ballots in their own language.

-To have access to the polling station and adequate assistance, which will not interfere with their right to cast a free and secret ballot.

States are under an obligation to:

-Ensure security for every individual involved in the elections.

-Ensure that vulnerable voters are able to cast their vote in free and fair procedure.

-Restrain from any type of intimidation.

-Suppress family, group, proxy and multiple voting.

-Ensure the integrity and transparency of e-voting.

Voting

-All sensitive material is adequately protected.

-The polling station's set up simultaneously ensures secrecy of the vote and the transparency of voting.

-Voting is conducted in an orderly manner and, in the absence of unauthorized persons, weapons or other objects that can endanger the voting. All voters are given a chance to cast their vote.

-Police cannot enter the polling station unless called by the polling board in case of disorder or violence.

Candidates

-Have their party representatives observe the voting, electoral boards' decision-making, counting and tallying of results.

-Immediately complain about noticed irregularities in the voting and request their termination.

Election administration

-Is vigilant to all attempts to rig elections. It conducts regular inspections in the polling stations and cooperates with the police regarding security-related matters.

-Provides opportunities and effective remedies to all voters unable to cast their vote.

-Effectively makes decisions, communicates and remains accessible to all involved in the elections. It provides guidance with respect to legislation and procedures connected with the election.

-Takes care of logistics and secures the storage and distribution of election materials.

-Supervises and disciplines lower levels of electoral administration.

Counting

-Counting of votes is done transparently and honestly.

-The official results are made public for each polling station.

-Candidates and observers have access to the minutes and results from the voting.

-The results are promptly delivered to a higher competent body for tallying.

<u>Post-elections</u>

Electoral administration

-Electoral results are tallied honestly and pronounced publicly, with no delay.

-Decides promptly on election complaints in a transparent procedure open to the public. It gives equal chances to all parties involved to provide their arguments and adduce evidence. The decisions relating to elections and election disputes are reasoned and well-justified.

-Declares the official electoral results with the shortest possible delay.

Electoral results

-In case of rigged elections, electoral results shall be annulled for the constituency or part of it where an illegal activity occurred.

-If electoral results are annulled, they must be repeated regardless of their impact on the electoral results. The elections will also be repeated if the voting was interrupted or did not take place at all.

Legal remedies

-There is an effective and adequate remedy to challenge the election results.

-Judicial appeals and complaints are dealt with fairly and in a timely manner in line with the requirement to publish the results as soon as possible.

-Election-related criminal offences are detected, promptly investigated and successfully prosecuted, which results in conviction and punishment of the perpetrators.

Mandate Entrusted to a Winning Candidate

-Electoral office is occupied by the winning candidate until the expiration of the elected office, except for valid legal reasons.

-Any attempts at post-electoral violence are effectively prevented and suppressed.

The above exercise is not just a simple summary or re-classification of the election standards as they stand in various European organizations. It is rather a merger of the election standards of the CoE, OSCE and EU, which also includes an emerging standard of meaningful representation. The above concrete election standards define the scope and substance of each theoretical principle declared in the international documents. Therefore, the common election standards in Europe should be seen as a practical tool for harmonious application of the Europe-wide electoral principles in national and supranational elections. They give a common key to the interpretation of the common principles of "free and fair elections" to the governments (organizing the elections), the opposition and the voters, on one side, as well as to the international and local election observers on the other side.

The discussion now turns to the specific standards elaborated above, as follows:

Distillation of the specific election standards offered by the three European organizations in order to conceptualize their avid version, deliberately omits a specific type of electoral system foreseen in the EP elections, for the following reasons: -firstly, not all of the countries bound by the European election standards elaborated by the CoE and OSCE belong to the

European continent; and -secondly, huge dissimilarities exist in terms of political, cultural and legal heritage even among the countries from the European continent.

However, the maximal 5% electoral threshold foreseen in the EU standards should be kept as one of the elements of the "free and fair" election paradigm in Europe, although it has not been explicitly mentioned in the OSCE or CoE standards. The main argument in its favor starts from the premise that the countries bound by the European standards are plural societies. Without putting limits on electoral thresholds, the plurality of the societies may not be reflected in the political decision-making. However, the contemporary political, human rights and legal processes advocate for greater inclusion of minority groups via free and fair elections.

A curious case is the observance of the equality suffrage, or rather a lack of it, in the EP elections. The case may be that there is a big difference in the votes by which the MPs from various EU states are elected, although they perform the same function in the same institution. Digressive proportionality also adds to the curiosity: is it possible to ensure equal suffrage in the EP, and how? Another perplexing case is the impossibility of standing as an individual candidate in the EP elections, which not only runs contrary to the OSCE and CoE election standards, but also to the non-discrimination embodied in the *acquis communautaire*. A hypothetical ECtHR scrutiny might prompt a change in this regard.

Whereas there are no specific EU rules for the electoral franchise, except "the non-nationals' universal right to vote", EU countries must abide by the OSCE and CoE relevant standards, due to their triple membership. The OSCE, for its part, has been borrowing from the CoE standards regarding the electoral campaign financing (public and private funding), electoral administration, and access to media. The OSCE commitments, for their part, explicitly require genuine elections as the basis of the legitimacy of government, the winning candidate occupying the office, and an environment conducive to political campaigning. The OSCE electoral commitments are spread out in its various documents and do not contain details on certain common principles that are set out in the CoE Code of Good Practice in Electoral Matters. For example, the latter devotes more attention to local and regional elections and specifies the voting requirements and counting procedures in detail.

III. European Regional Organizations Developing Standards in the Election Field

Delimitation of electoral boundaries favoring minority representation is still fragile and has not been encompassed, as such, in the ECtHR corpus of interpretative election standards. By contrast, the ECtHR is the sole body that supported the idea that there was a conflict of interest when an electoral candidate holds a position allowing influence over public media. An ownership of a decisive share in private media has not been mentioned anywhere as an obstacle to stand for elections.

Effective and adequate legal remedies in all electoral spheres represent a target for all sets of the European election standards. However, this requirement needs to be translated into concrete terms, especially for the media rules violations. Whereas the media are subject to sanctions, the electoral candidate still benefits from the violation. The same is valid for a violation of campaign financing rules, unless national law effectively and fairly enforces a prohibition to occupy an elected office won by breaking the law. The enforcement of punitive provisions, effective sanctions and perseverance to combat impunity does not agree with according amnesty to election-related offenders. Such amnesty is usually accorded to the "party soldiers" who sacrifice themselves in the name of electoral victory. However, it is acknowledged that a prohibition on granting amnesty for election related offences has not yet been formulated as a clear electoral standard.

Although the election observation commitments have not been included in the CoE and the EU sets of electoral commitments, the fact remains that these organizations make electoral observation a part of their practice. The judicial remedy requirement and "zero tolerance" for impunity in electoral cases are indirectly imposed on the EU member states for the EP elections, via their OSCE and CoE memberships. This assumption can be verified in practice only if country-by-country analyses are conducted about their valid international and national electoral rules.

Finally, the above-proposed specific standards may vary in their impact on the EU, due to this organization's *sui generis* nature. European harmonized standards in the electoral field will *de facto* result in greater approximation of the election rules for all types of elections in the EU countries, the EP elections included. It will represent a follow-up to the OSCE/ODIHR recommendations with respect to the EP elections. Such *de minimus,* standards will not prevent the EU from elaborating more detailed standards in the specific electoral areas as the need may be. At any rate, the EU being a champion of democracy on the European continent cannot allow itself to conduct elections under lower standards than those valid for the OSCE and CoE member states.

III. EUROPEAN SCRUTINY OVER IMPLEMENTATION OF ELECTION STANDARDS

It is easier to set standards than to observe them. The CoE and the OSCE are two pillars on which the enforcement of European election standards within the European boundaries lie. The EU represents the third pillar, considering the importance of the European integration processes on the continent.

When the aggregate of the European election-mandated bodies is scrutinized, it comes to light that various bodies within a single organization have a range of mandates and tools at their disposal. The current practice involves election observations, examination of individual applications, technical assistance, legislative assessments, and political dialogues with the governments, thus shaping the states' behavior when "free and fair elections" are at stake.

The outcome that the CoE, OSCE and EU seek to achieve on the basis of the devolved powers by the states are "free and fair elections" in Europe. In absence of a unified approach to what is considered "free and fair", they operate in line with their instruments' standards.

The ECtHR, as a judicial body, is neither a special court for election cases, nor does it foresee specific resources or remedies for the election-related cases. Therefore, the generic problems that the ECtHR faces on daily basis also represent a constraint for election cases. The ECtHR statistics reveal an influx of applications, which undoubtedly causes great difficulties in promptly processing cases. Of course, the most effective and least costly way would consist of full enforcement of the ECHR by the states.

The remedies awarded by the ECtHR include monetary compensation, while individual and general measures for rectifying injustice are left to the discretion of the country concerned. Therefore, they do not fit best the electoral context, as the ECtHR corrects the violation, *ex-post*, within the limited scope of its competence. Moreover, the ECtHR also has difficulties with the enforcement of its judgments. On one hand, it appears that enforcement lacks sufficient safeguards to ensure the full impact of the judgments of the ECtHR.[149] On the other hand, there are some symptoms of crises for the enforcement as even founding states like

---

[149] Steiner, Alston, International Human Rights in Context, Law, Politics, Morals (2nd edition) (2000) p. 803.

III. European Scrutiny over Implementation of Election Standards

France or the United Kingdom[150] are sometimes reluctant to enforce a judgment. The PACE regularly deals with the issue of the enforcement of the ECtHR judgments, recognizing that the problem of the lack of enforcement might even jeopardize the whole system for the protection of human rights.

The OSCE/ODIHR is the watchdog of elections in Europe, although its mandate captures more than "free and fair elections". Its election observation missions operate under the assumption of professionalism, impartiality and competence. However, it seems that its teeth are not sharp enough. In particular, the follow-up to its electoral observation reports and recommendations has been identified as a challenge,[151] in addition to the problems with certain OSCE member states objecting to its methodology and selection of countries to be observed. In addition, it appears that OSCE/ODIHR is restraint also due to limited resources and funds. However, any effective follow-up must be done by the participating States, with OSCE/ODIHR only assisting in that process by providing their expertise and support.

The OSCE PA, which is composed of parliamentarians from the OSCE participating states, focuses on short-term observation. Pursuant to the 1997 Cooperation Agreement with the ODIHR, the OSCE PA assumes a political leadership role, whereas the ODIHR assesses elections on the basis of technocratic methods.

The PACE, a deliberative body of the CoE, consists of delegations of members of national parliaments. Among its other duties, it observes parliamentary and presidential elections in cooperation with OSCE/ODIHR and the EU PA. Unlike the OSCE/ODIHR election observation, which focuses on the technical evaluation, the PACE focuses also on the assessment of the political situation. If an applicant country refuses to accept PACE's election observation mission, its applicant's process can be adjourned in the CoE!

The bodies that do not observe elections for their quality, but are entrusted with monitoring and reporting about specific aspects of electoral legislation and practice, comprise GRECO and the European Commission for Democracy through Law (the VC). The former serves the

---

[150] Implementation of Judgments of the European Court of Human Rights, Progress Report, Parliamentary Assembly (2009) As/Jur (2009) 36 at <http: //www.coe.int>.
[151] OSCE/ODIHR, The Annex to Common Responsibility Commitments and Implementation (2006) Note Verbale No. 257/06; the 2009 Vilnius Declaration of the OSCE Parliamentary Assembly, Resolution on Election Observation the OSCE, AS(0) D1E at <http://www.osce.org>.

III. European Scrutiny over Implementation of Election Standards

CoE member states to assure a meaningful follow-up to the common rules against corruption in the funding of political parties and electoral campaigns. The latter, on other hand, is in charge with the formulation and promotion of European election standards, as well as of legislative assessments. Since 2002, most of its activities are jointly executed with the Council for Democratic Elections, which also has representatives from the CLRAE and PACE.

The results of the above examination of the relevant election protection mechanisms on the supply side point out to the same drawbacks, i.e., all these bodies struggle with a lack of resources and funds, lengthy and untimely procedures contributing to the loss of momentum, and a lack of opportunity for effective follow-up to their decisions/recommendations. The lack of mandate and the restraint coming from the principle of sovereignty of the states also have a role to play in this regard. In some instances, election observation has been seriously challenged by some states, mostly along west-east lines. They, *inter alia,* object that it was not clear against which international election standards the elections were assessed, because the criteria were not clearly set out in the report.

Furthermore, all examined organizations in their key documents mention their preferences for democracy, protection of human rights and the rule of law, but the question remains how to make a bridge between the democratic values and principles and the practice in the international/regional organizations? The lack of an effective mechanism for the responsibility of international organizations is not helping the better elaboration of internal democratic principles.[152] Nevertheless, in fact, there are attempts these organizations to control each other depending on who their member states are. From the viewpoint of traditional international law, the states are the key actors in these organizations, so the decisions are based on their political will. However, international organizations should serve as an example for what they stand for, thereby increasing their effectiveness when supporting the states in their democratization efforts. There must be more than a mere coincidence between the effectiveness of the international organization supporting "free and fair elections" and the perceived level of democracy on whose basis that organization operates. Greater transparency, support for diversity, accountability, non-discrimination and effective remedy are among the elements of the inter-governmental organizations' internal democracy.

---

[152] Draft Articles on Responsibility of International Organizations, International Law Commission, adopted by the International Law Commission at its sixty-third session, in 2011.

III. European Scrutiny over Implementation of Election Standards

Democratic principles for the functioning of the inter-governmental organizations go hand in hand with globalization.

The above approach is also in balance with the international principle of the state sovereignty, taking into consideration that international organizations represent a space for expression of competing interests and political wills. It is even more important in view of the fact that the biggest demand for democratization assistance comes from the countries who are usually not big contributors, do not have much power in decision-making, and sometimes are not even a member of the international organization. The states who are the biggest consumers of the democratization assistance, as a rule lack, a developed democratic capacity. Elections cannot be considered sufficient for a society to be considered democratic, as it could lead to a sustainable survival of competitive authoritarianisms. Therefore, high hopes are put in the international level. In such cases, the international factor contributes a great deal to the liberalization of election outcomes. [153] An adequate answer to the expectations and public confidence is an important goal for the inter-governmental organizations, in view of its audience costs.

The efficiency and the effectiveness of electoral assistance are also undermined by the demand side. In particular, states may not be willing to invite international observers to observe their elections, as there is no mandatory duty for the states to invite international election observers.[154] States may also impose many obstacles to the effect that any meaningful observation of elections is impossible, or object when it is only one person (politician/expert) making the assessment. States might not articulate well the needed assistance, or may not coordinate well the foreign election's aid with the ramifications being a waste of international funds and resources, and ineffective assistance. The recipient-state may also not put sufficient trust in the regional supervisory mechanism, accusing it of bias on the grounds of its composition, hidden agendas, a lack of expertise and methodology, or a privileged treatment of some states.[155]

---

[153] Levitsky, Way Autocracy by Democratic Rules: The Dynamics of Competitive Authoritarianism in the Post Cold War Era (rev. 2003) p. 7.
[154] D'Amato, International Law Anthology (1994) p. 371.
[155] Van der Linden, Conclusions of the President of the Parliamentary Assembly of the CoE, 15-16 February (2007) pp. 3, 12, 22, 29, 30, 43-47 at <http//www.coe.int>.

III. European Scrutiny over Implementation of Election Standards

In view of the above, the need for a cooperative approach and practice of all these bodies is evident, with the aim of having international community speak with a single voice.[156] Such a reaction must be balanced by impartiality, professionalism and ascertained facts.

For the OSCE/ODIHR, the internal cooperation between ODIHR and the OSCE PA is needed in order to avoid issuing diverging assessments of the observed elections, holding parallel press conferences and competing for media attention. Nevertheless, their mutual cooperation and coordination resulted in a number of problems, including: a lack of joint statements for the US presidential and congressional elections; PA claiming that ODIHR did not comply with the 1997 key provisions and failed to share the complete information; did not abide by the principles of transparency and accountability; applied double standards in the election observation; and criticized the ODIHR methodology as not being flexible enough to apply to all participating states. Paradoxically, the cooperation between ODIHR and external partners, like the CoE seems to be perceived as more beneficial. The ODIHR findings are closely coordinated with the EOMs from the CoE Parliamentary Assembly and the CLRAE, respectively in spite of sporadic problems, which are more connected with logistics. As to the EU, in addition to funding election-related activities, its member countries[157] along with the US, second the largest number of election observers in ODIHR.

Interchange between the OSCE field operations and the UN agencies, e.g., the UNDP, sometimes results in duplication of efforts and missed opportunities for joint lobbying with the respective government. Although the OSCE documents repeatedly request the participating states to ratify the UN Bill of Rights, the CEDAW and the CERD, all of which build the body of international election standards, the UN documents are used only in rare cases. Although a cooperation agreement has been signed with the OHCHR that foresees regular consultations, joint work and initiatives, the interviewed officials from the OSCE/ODIHR never mentioned it. In general, it appears that there was no cooperation between them and the UN in the election field, perhaps because of a lack of joint interest to cooperate at the European level.

---

[156] Haller, Election Observation by the Parliamentary Assembly of the CoE (PACE) (…) pp. 7-8 at <http://www.coe.int>.
[157] Bailes, Haine, Lachowski, Reflections on the OSCE-EU Relationship, OSCE Yearbook (2007) p. 77 at <http://www.coe.int>.

III. European Scrutiny over Implementation of Election Standards

In sum, the above cases illustrate the controversial and politicized background sometimes even full of security threats, in which election observation takes place. This is not only with respect to who will win the power, but also about the direction and future of the country in view of the complex global political environment. It goes without saying that observation of elections must be carefully planned and conducted in consideration of the political environment and its broader context. A lack of cooperation and coordination between international organizations, which may result in different assessments of elections, represents a great danger, as it can only lead to a loss of credibility and to the impossibility of any meaningful election observation being carried out by international observers. In addition, the overlapping mandates of different bodies increase the costs, while the competition may replace the desired coordination.[158] In some countries where the elections have been observed for more than 15 years, they still continue to be flawed. Thus, the practice does not support the view that election observation is a sufficient tool for ensuring clean elections.

Although it may be argued that the existing review mechanisms are not weak and that they have a sufficiently effective cumulative effect when aggregated, it is clear that there is a problem regarding the protection of election rights in Europe. In short, the assessment of elections, election legislation and protection of election rights is not lacking at the European level, judging by the wealth of organizations committed to these goals. What is lacking is the effective follow-up of these bodies' reports and recommendations, which in turn will also prevent the election irregularities from re-occurring. The follow-up to the reports from the election observation missions and election legislation assessments is marginalized if there is no political will of both: the state and the inter-governmental organization, to secure the implementation of the most important recommendations.

In addition, a successful electoral reform is constrained by the following factors: a) the violation of various election standards might not have the same degree of seriousness, with the states picking and choosing which ones to remedy; b) the reforms' elevated costs burden the country and the organization; c) there are insufficient funds and expertise; d) plural societies tend to have problems that cannot be easily solved through "free and fair elections"; e) a balanced electoral assistance is lacking due to deficient coordination and cooperation at the international level and a lack of a meaningful dialogue with the relevant country, f) there

---

[158] Steiner, Alston, International Human Rights in Context, Law, Politics, Morals (2nd edition) (2000) p. 793.

is low public awareness about the electoral reform needed, g) there is a lack of local infrastructure (political parties, NGOs) supporting the electoral reform and h) there is no appropriate penalty in case of a breach of international electoral rules, like for example suspension of the relevant international organization's membership.

A meaningful follow-up may have as constraints or as boosters a number of political considerations shaping its form, when a particular country is concerned. At any rate, it is the domestic institutions that should provide the appropriate response to the detected weaknesses and later implement what has been internationally decided.

IV. EUROPEAN ELECTION STANDARDS IN NATIONAL JURISDICTIONS: A COMPARISON

1. Background

There are three parallel worlds of election standards in Europe: the CoE world, the OSCE world and the EU world. While most of the electoral worlds contain, *ergo omnes,* electoral obligations, for some of the CoE electoral sub-worlds the legal value of the standards and their specifities differ depending on the relevant instrument.

By including national electoral jurisdictions, a big picture of the interplay between the international mechanisms, domestic laws and institutions emerges. Due consideration is given to the fact that the paradigm of "free and fair elections" has been first developed in the "old democracies" and then disseminated through international organizations. Therefore, the analysis of this part is firmly based on the premise that the European standards in the election field are derived from the electoral rules of the consolidated democracies, which first started to practice electoral democracy (see the diagram below).

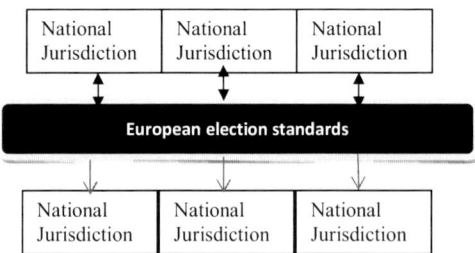

Since the states accumulate the electoral obligations and they are the main doers in the electoral world, this part examines electoral legislation and institutions of a group of states bound by the European values. The principles and specific standards identified in the study serve as the units of analysis in order to compare a selected diversified sample of states. One of the criteria for the sample selection is democratic governance. Still, the selected states vary in terms of history, tradition, membership in the relevant organizations and political organization of the society.

IV. European Election Standards in National Jurisdictions: A Comparison

The sample comprises two ex-Yugoslav republics: Macedonia and Slovenia; four "old democracies": France, Belgium, Switzerland and UK; and two ex-USSR countries: Ukraine and Azerbaijan, and EU four member states: Belgium, France, Slovenia and UK. The most ethnically homogeneous countries are Azerbaijan and Slovenia. Only Macedonia and Azerbaijan underwent an inter-ethnic conflict after 1990. Azerbaijan is included in the sample to illustrate the application of the European standards to a non-European country.

2. National Legislation - Source of Election Standards

The paradigm of "free and fair elections" at the national level, embodies the electoral principles of universal, fair, equal, regular, direct and genuine elections. These principles, which safeguard democracy, are reflected in the legislation of all states examined with certain variations and differences in view of the countries' particular circumstances.

There is high level of consistency with respect to the general electoral principles in the selected sample. The principles of equal, regular, direct, universal and secret are announced at the constitutional level, thus safeguarded by the highest legal act.[159] The principle of free elections has been directly mentioned only in the Macedonian[160] and Ukrainian[161] constitutions, whereas in France its substance is conveyed through guaranteed freedom of expression of the political parties.[162]

As to the differences and variations of the constitutional paradigms, there are certain principles set out in the individual constitutions, which may serve as a model for other countries. The Belgian Constitution detailing out the equality principle in elections, requires re-assessment and re-adjustment of the electoral boundaries every 10 years.[163] Thus, the equal opportunity principle to be elected and to elect has received a constitutional guarantee.

As to the bundle of electoral rights connected with the principle of a "meaningful representation", several constitutions reflect the requirement for political representation of

---

[159] The Federal Constitution of Switzerland is the only exception. In absence of codified constitution the UK has not been included in this group.
[160] Article 22.
[161] Article 71.
[162] French Constitution, Article 4.
[163] Article 63, paragraph 3.

women.[164] Namely, the most homogeneous country-Slovenia, is the one that foresees increased electoral guarantees for certain minorities,[165] along with Belgium for the EP elections. The political plurality principle and equitable representation of parties have been mirrored only in the French Constitution,[166] despite being a core element of true democracy.

The electoral rights converge on the points of age qualifications for the voters[167] and citizenship requirements.[168] Furthermore, whereas horizontally disfranchisement is imposed due to a general lack of legal or mental capacity as established by the court,[169] no individualization is required when voting rights are at stake. Several countries have stricter conditions for certain offices, i.e., higher age limit. Azerbaijan deprives its citizens with a dual citizenship from passive electoral rights, which is incompatible with the ECHR requirements. Ukraine imposes a 5-year residence requirement for becoming an elected MP, which is incompatible with the paragraph c. iii. and iv. of the Code of Good Practice in Electoral Matters. The incompatibility uncovers itself on the points of the type of elections for which a residence requirement is acceptable, as well as its length.

The generated national principles further branch out in various pieces of electoral legislation. The legislation regulates panoply of elections depending on the country's political and electoral system.

The hypothetical European election standards, as proposed in the doctoral dissertation, serve herein as a measuring tool in order to avoid several rounds of electoral assessments by various organizational sets of standards. In their role of an electoral performance indicator, they dissipate the dilemma about which standard or set of standards is applicable. Furthermore, they displace the focus of the standards from their persuasive power to their substance in the function of "free and fair elections". When an electoral assessment is carried out by a specific organization or by its body, the key source of the electoral rules is clear.

---

[164] Electoral justice for women has been guaranteed directly by France, Belgium and Slovenia (Articles 1, 11-bis and 43, respectively) and indirectly by Ukraine (Article 24).

[165] Article 64 of the Slovenian Constitution.

[166] Article 4.

[167] Article 70 of the Ukrainian Constitution, Article 136 of the Swiss Constitution, Article 61 of the Belgian Constitution, Article 43 of the Slovenian Constitution, Article 3 of the French Constitution and Article 22 of the Macedonian Constitution. For Azerbaijan, the age requirement is stipulated in Article 12 of the Electoral Code.

[168] Article 70 of the Ukrainian Constitution, Article 136 of the Swiss Constitution, Article 61 of the Belgian Constitution, Article 43 of the Slovenian Constitution, Article 22 of the Macedonian Constitution, Article 56 of the Azerbaijani Constitution and Article 3 of the French Constitution.

[169] Article 70 of the Ukrainian Constitution, Article 61 of the Belgian Constitution, Article 56 of the Azerbaijani Constitution, Article 22 of the Macedonian Constitution and Article 3 of the French Constitution.

IV. European Election Standards in National Jurisdictions: A Comparison

However, when the assessment is done by another actor, preferring one set of standards to another may entail arbitrariness. The need to harmonize the existing standards is yet another argument for elaborating common European standards by the three main stakeholders: the CoE, EU and OSCE.

The comparison among the selected countries is primarily based on national legislation and on the assessments of the countries' elections made by the CoE and OSCE bodies. On the facts extracted from the above-mentioned sources, the proposed election standards are applied while using electoral cycle approach, as follows:

Pre-election phase

Electoral system and law: - *Direct regular elections* of at least one chamber in the legislature is a common feature of all countries under examination. Since international obligations do not demand a specific electoral system or method, the countries employ different electoral systems. For example, in Macedonia the general elections are held in six constituencies under the proportional system with closed candidates' lists, except for out-of-country voting. Similar to Macedonia, Belgium uses the proportional electoral systems.[170] In Slovenia, eighty-eight MPs in the National Assembly are elected in 8 constituencies, again under the proportional representation system, with the elements of the majority system. Unlike Macedonia, which does not foresee an electoral threshold, Slovenian legislation prescribes a 4% threshold. In the latter country, due regard is given to the personalization of voters, i.e., ensuring the influence of the voters in the choice of candidates. Whereas in Macedonia (for the post-conflict period), one of the main impetus to change the law also came from the international community in view of the election observation reports, the Slovenian experience showed that the main drive in modeling Slovenian legislation was with the political parties. As to the reminder of the countries from the sample, Switzerland and Ukraine use mixed electoral systems. The plurality model is used in the UK and Azerbaijan, whereas France applies the majority electoral system with two rounds.[171] The EU member countries use different variations of the proportional electoral system for the EP elections.

---

[170] Belgian Constitution, Article 62.
[171] IPU database accessed on 18 July 2013 at <http://www.ipu.org>.

IV. European Election Standards in National Jurisdictions: A Comparison

-In all subjects that have undergone an examination, *the electoral intervals* for electing the legislature do not exceed a 5-year period of time. Switzerland, along with the two hereditary monarchies, is an exception to direct presidential elections. The sub-national levels of government in a number of countries have a mandate exceeding 5 years.[172] All countries hold periodic direct mayoral elections, except for Belgium.

-As to the different limbs of the requirement for a *meaningful representation*, the results of the examination show the following:

Regarding its first limb, none of the examined countries, which uses a proportional representation system, has a legal election threshold higher than 5%.

As to the second limb, Switzerland and Azerbaijan do not prescribe affirmative measures for women, or if measures are prescribed their concretization is lacking, which is precisely the case of Ukraine.[173] France is a positive example in this regard, as direct public funding is conditioned with the promotion of women candidates.[174] Slovenia requires an equitable representation of women candidates on the candidates' lists. Its Administrative Court[175] reviewed a case whereby the candidates' list did not fulfill the legal requirements, as one of the nominated female candidates was not a resident of the municipality. The MEC deleted the next male candidate on the candidates' list, so that the legal requirement for gender equitable representation was fulfilled. The complainant claimed that the MEC was not allowed to correct the candidates' list. Since the complainant did not submit any evidence that it tried to correct the list within the legal deadline, the lawsuit was dismissed by the Administrative Court. Commenting on the case, it is peculiar for the MEC to decide who should be a candidate on the candidates' list based upon the gender requirement. It was the duty of the MEC to ask the candidates' list submitter who should stay or be deleted from the list of candidates, in view of their right to correct candidates' list. Therefore, it appears that the MEC acted outside its competence without a proper justification.

---

[172] Council of European Municipalities and Regions, Local and Regional Government in Europe, Structures and Competences (2012) pp. 6, 19, 47, 53.
[173] Quotaproject at <http://www.quotaproject.org>.
[174] Idea International at <http://www.idea.int> accessed on 6 July 2013.
[175] Sodba U 520/2006.

IV. European Election Standards in National Jurisdictions: A Comparison

The countries use various ways to achieve the minority representation, ranging from specifically tailored constituencies to electoral systems and reserved seats. For instance, in Slovenia, the members of the Italian and Hungarian ethnic groups can cast two votes. Double voting rights are considered as a measure of positive discrimination. According to the data of 2002 Census[176] Italians make up 0.11% and Hungarians 0.32% of the population. They are accorded 1 reserved seat per ethnic group at the National Assembly in order to enable their greater participation in public affairs. However, Roma are not accorded the same right, although their proportion of 0.17% of the total population is slightly higher than the proportion of Italians. In order to allow the Roma, as a vulnerable group, to enhance their participation in public affairs, it is recommended to accord them with a reserved seat at the National Assembly.[177]

Azerbaijan and Ukraine still have to work on promotion and participation of minorities judging according to the ODIHR election reports. Article 11 of the Belgian Federal Constitution even proscribes discrimination of ideological and philosophical minorities in the enjoyment of their political rights. Such broad protection of the "atypical minorities" may serve as a model for other countries, as it feeds the never-ending debate about how to improve the conditions of human society.

The third limb refers to the impossibility of democracy to function only with one choice at the disposal of the voters. The important function that the opposition plays, and its protection, is underscored only in the French Constitution.[178] In the UK, a concrete measure requires that only the parliamentary opposition receive public funds to perform its duties.[179]

Finally, the meaningful representation standard is connected with meaningful participation. However, only Belgium prescribes compulsory voting. The rest of the countries struggle with lower turnout rates ranging between 49.10% and 65.77% for parliamentary elections. By comparison, there is a higher turnout of voters in the presidential elections in France, Ukraine and Azerbaijan, with the exception of the two ex-Yugoslav republics, which in fact are the only ones in this group with a parliamentary system. On the other side, for the EP elections,

---

[176] Official web site of the Statistical Office of Slovenia at <http://www.stat.si>.
[177] CERD Annual Report A/65/18, pp. 117-118.
[178] Article 4, paragraph 3 of the French Constitution stipulates the following: "Statutes shall guarantee the expression of diverse opinions and the equitable participation of political parties and groups in the democratic life of the Nation."
[179] GRECO, Evaluation Report on UK on Transparency of Party Funding, Third Evaluation Report (2007) p. 7.

the EU members struggle with the voter turnout as low as 28.33% in Slovenia, 34.48% in the UK and 40.63% in France[180], indicating the disinterested voters' phenomena with respect to European issues.

-As to the *law-making* in the context of election, the following countries still struggle with the application of the electoral law-making standards:

The Macedonian election law and electoral system have changed often, which may indicate a superficial law-making process.[181] The changes sometimes occurred a few months before elections, which is incompatible with the international election standards. In some instances, neither the ruling coalition nor the opposition were interested in amending the Election Code, e.g., regarding transparency of electoral campaign funding, as recommended by ODIHR. In short, the political will was missing to adopt some key amendments in order to harmonize the legislation with international election standards, which had ramifications on the law-making process. Still, these frequent legislative changes, coupled with the assistance offered by the civil sector in the country and the international factor, contributed to slow but steady improvements of the election legislation.

It appears that Ukraine and Azerbaijan should also improve their electoral law-making in an inclusive and transparent process.[182] In Slovenia, although there is a vibrant civil sector with a keen interest in elections that lobbies for a greater inclusion of disabled persons, it appears that its prompt and systematic inclusion in the law-making process is somehow lacking. The possibility to publicly comment on electoral drafts is necessary, but not a sufficient condition for transparent law-making.

The UK has undertaken an electoral reform with clear deadlines in reply to the ODIHR recommendation to consolidate the electoral legislation. In short, the focus for the follow-up by the countries should be on the usefulness of the recommendations and not on devising the ways how to by-pass them.

---

[180] Idea International at <http://www.idea.int/vt/countryview.cfm?id=42:// accessed on 2 August 2013.
[181] Coalition All For Fair Trials, Corruption Trial Monitoring Programme in the Republic of Macedonia (2008) p. 17.
[182] The OSCE/ODIHR Election Observation Reports on Ukrainian 2012 Parliamentary Elections, p. 7; the OSCE/ODIHR Azerbaijani 2010 Parliamentary Elections, pp. 5, 24.

IV. European Election Standards in National Jurisdictions: A Comparison

On a separate note, the differences in the law-making traditions are reflected in the electoral legislation of the countries from the sample. For instance, Azerbaijan and Ukraine include great detail in their electoral legislation, without leaving much space for secondary legislation. The legislative drafting method in Slovenia and Macedonia is similar, with a difference that the latter codified the legislation in the Electoral Code upon the recommendation of the OSCE/ODIHR. Electoral legislation has been also codified in Azerbaijan, Belgium and France. However, in Belgium some specific electoral matters, like the electoral campaign funding, or automatic vote remain uncodified. It does not appear that electoral codification is necessary as long as the relevant laws are consistent, clear and precise.

Voters: - While the selected countries have firmly implanted the electoral principle of the *universal vote*, its translation into electoral rules varies in terms of qualifying criteria. The prisoners' vote dilemma in the UK unfolded from the ECtHR's scrutiny over the prisoners' disenfranchisement and from the OSCE/ODIHR election observation report. The Scottish Parliament rejected the proposal to alleviate the blanket ban for prisoners, whereas the proposal to allow a 16-year old youth to vote gained its support.[183] No other country from the sample allows children's vote in elections.

As to the non-nationals' voting rights, the table of ratification indicates that none of the examined countries has ratified the Convention on the Participation of Foreigners in Public Life at Local Level. Nonetheless, except for Macedonia, Ukraine and France the reminder of the countries foresees some type of a third country's non-national voting, subject to various residency requirements. Azerbaijan explicitly foresees voting rights for stateless persons in local, presidential and general elections. Slovenia has also made a breakthrough regarding residents from ex-Yugoslavia, including stateless persons.[184] The EU members grant election rights to non-nationals in possession of EU citizenship.

Inclusion of persons with mental impairment in public life is an obligation, which has been undertaken internationally by all the countries from the sample, except for Switzerland. For instance, in Azerbaijan the court decides on active election right of a person with mental

---

[183] Scottish Prisoners Challenge Ban on Voting in Independence Referendum, The Guardian, press release, 28 June 2013.
[184] Accetto, Access to Electoral Rights Slovenia (2013) pp. 1-2.

impairment.[185] In Slovenia, a voter must not be fully incapacitated or placed in a guardianship, and he must understand the meaning and importance of elections for the active election right. In Belgium, a person with a mental impairment can cast a vote, if he or she is not interned, if he or she is not protected in the same way as a minor younger than 15 years, or he or she has not been incapacitated.

- A remedy for an incomplete or improper *voters' registration* as it stands in the national legislations does not seem to pose any problem, nor does the requirement for maintaining and keeping voters' lists, as defined in the laws. However, the states have been struggling to preserve in practice the principles of having complete and accurate voters' lists. For example, the OSCE/ODIHR has noted as a weakness the UK's practice of allowing voters' registration without a proper identification. Since the voters' identification is just a means to compile and maintain voters' lists, and if the needed accuracy and completeness of the voters' lists can be achieved in another way, (for example by data cross checking) there might be no need to require a voters' identification. Simultaneously, while other selected countries do not seem to have, *per se,* the voters' identification problem, the OSCE/ODIHR detected a number of other problems in this area. In this context, the duty to protect personal date from the voters' lists from abuse[186] seems shared by all states to various extents. Another practice that can be shared comes from Belgium: -voters can be added or deleted from the list of electors one day before Election Day, which allows for a greater use without abuse of the voting rights.

- *Informed and educated voters* must be supported by the state. Whereas all countries stipulate an obligation for voters' education; the so-called "old democracies" minus Belgium, conduct continuous voters' education. The continuous voters' education certainly reflects good electoral practice, whose seed should be planted in other countries that put their trust in the democratic system of governance.

In 1996, the Slovenian Law on National Assembly Elections was abrogated in part, as it did not foresee publication of the national candidates' lists in the media and at the polling stations. As a consequence, the voters only knew the competing parties, but not the party

---

[185] Report of the Republic of Azerbaijan to the CRPD Committee on Article 29.
[186] The 2007 Ukrainian Law on State Voters' Registration, the 2008 Electoral Code of the Republic of Azerbaijan; OSCE/ODIHR, Komentar na Izborniot Zakonik (2009) p. 98; UK Managing Electoral Registration in Great Britain, Guidance for Electoral Registration Officers (2013) p. 43; Venice Commission and OSCE/ODIHR Joint Opinion on the Electoral Code of Macedonia (2013) p. 5 at <http://www.coe.int>.

candidates, meaning that the well-informed voters' element was lacking. The court found that one of the three criteria for direct elections had not been fulfilled, since the national candidates' lists were not public. Not only did the right to elect candidates rest with political parties, but the voters were not even given access to key information for elections, i.e., to which personage they might delegate their sovereign rights. The court's decision was taken in the right direction, since a system that does not promote transparency in matters, such as electoral candidates, misses an important feature of democracy.

- Another state's duty, i.e., the *delimitation of the boundaries* seems problematic in Ukraine. Not only because the magnitude of the constituencies may vary up to 12%, but also because of its impact on the representativeness of the minorities in Ukraine, as concluded by IFES. In Macedonia, the equality of the vote controversy is connected with the diaspora vote, as those MPs may be elected with a considerably smaller number of votes, and the size of the electoral districts is defined in terms of continents. In Slovenia, the Constitutional Court quashed two decisions of municipal councils defining the electoral units contrary to equal voting rights and ordered it to correct the irregularity in time for the next elections. In particular, the election units were not defined by the number of residents as required by law, and there was a substantial difference in numbers of the residents in various units.[187]

Candidates: - The oldest applicable document in this regard, the 1789 French Declaration of Human and Civil Rights declares merits-based *access to public offices based on equality*. After more than two hundred years, the qualifications to be nominated as an electoral candidate occupy a whole range of the eligibility spectrum. Its most restrictive interpretation is reflected in the Ukrainian law that foresees a 5-year residence requirement in order to become an MP.

- The *prisoners' nomination* for elections is yet another dilemma in the eligibility spectrum. A conviction for an election-related offence is a permissible restriction. Namely, in Azerbaijan and Ukraine, the imprisonment represents a temporary obstacle to stand in elections. Such a restriction is in place not only because of the moral aptitude, but also because of its impracticability. However, the incarceration of the opposition candidates

---

[187] U-I-381/98-8, Uradni List RS, no. 66/2000; Uradni List RS, no. 118/2004.

following a trial, which presumably did not comply with the fair trial standards, cannot fall under the above-mentioned exception.

By the same token, the Electoral Code of Azerbaijan gives an excessive power to the prosecution. In particular, it requires that no registered candidate be detained or convicted by the court in the absence of the prosecutors' consent. Commenting on this, it appears as though the prosecutor can interfere with the courts' dispensing justice. However, unless it is a minor offence, it is unclear how the courts would adjudicate a candidate without an indictment filed by the prosecution.[188] The Ukrainian Constitution stipulates that a person convicted for having committed an intentional crime cannot stand for parliamentary elections.[189] Such a general Constitutional provision, which does not specify the severity of crimes or their type, e.g., if they are election-related offences, will have to be applied in line with the proportionality and individualization principles, under an objective and reasonable rationale.

In Macedonia, the Constitutional Court[190] found a violation of the applicant's passive electoral right when it established that the electoral bodies rejected his nomination without updating information about the applicant's criminal record. This decision was rightfully adopted by the court, or else a candidate would have been deprived of his passive election right only due to a lack of information of the very body, which should have defended his election rights. In another Macedonian case, a winning candidate was sentenced to a prison sentence during elections, which resulted in a repeated election. In Slovenia, although a criminal conviction is not an obstacle to the passive election right, Article 9 of the Law on MPs prescribes a loss of mandate in case of conviction to an unconditional sentence of imprisonment of six or more months. In fact, such a criterion would also be an obstacle to running as an electoral candidate, as a mandate could not be verified in such a case. The current legal solution seems to be to impose a duty on the candidates' nominators to check if the above criterion has been fulfilled, which might prove difficult for verification.

Unlike Macedonia, Slovenia has never adopted a lustration law. This means that there are no criteria for the passive election right prohibiting an election candidate from standing in

---

[188] Article 70.4 of Azerbaijani Electoral Code. There is a similar provision regarding detention or indictment of EMB members, Article 27.
[189] Article 76.
[190] Constitutional Court decision No. 84/2009 adopted 10 February 2010.

elections, if he or she had collaborated with the ex-secret service to the detriment of human rights in the past.

Bankruptcy represents an additional reason to disqualify a person from standing in a UK election.[191]

- The incompatibility of the elected office with other types of offices ensues from a *separation of powers* doctrine.[192] The cumulation of offices is connected with the integrity and honesty of the peoples' representatives.[193] As a rule, elected office is incompatible with other elected offices, with judicial, military and civil servants' offices, with the police service and the EMBs membership. Other relevant incompatibilities extend to the category of religious officials who are banned from standing for election in Azerbaijan[194] and the UK.[195] The 2011 French Electoral Code prescribes ineligibility of, *inter alia,* rectors and inspectors of academia. In Macedonia, MPs are not only prohibited from cumulating functions, but also from executing profitable activities, as being an MP is a full-time job.[196]

The separation of powers doctrine also prohibits the use of administrative resources for campaigning purposes. However, despite the legal obligation to respect the separation between the state and a party, in Ukraine the OSCE/ODIHR detected an abuse of state resources. State and local officials were participating in electoral campaign.[197]

Regarding Macedonia, the efforts made to address this concern by way of legislative reform, were deemed insufficient according to ODIHR. The prevailing reasons lie in a lack of regulation for the ministers' campaigning during municipal elections and electoral disbursement of public funds before the official start of the campaign.

- A selection of candidates in the primaries, introduced in 2009 in France, represents a good example of *internal party democracy.* Internal party democracy is also promoted by the Slovenian model whereby the political parties are required by law to elect election candidates by secret vote. Still, no more candidates than the number of posts for which they compete are

---

[191] GRECO, Third Evaluation Round, Evaluation Report on UK on Transparency of Party Funding (2007) p. 4.
[192] Section 77 of the Venice Commission's Report on Democracy, Limitation of Mandates and Incompatibility of Political Functions (2013), Study no. 646 / 2011, CDL-AD(2012)027rev., p. 14.
[193] Idea International, Ten Years of Supporting Democracy Worldwide, pp. 69-70 at <http://www.idea.int>.
[194] The Azerbaijani Constitution revised in 2002, Article 56.
[195] GRECO, 4th Evaluation Round of UK, Corruption Prevention in respect of Members of Parliament, Judges and Prosecutors (2012) pp. 16-17.
[196] Article 8 of the Macedonian Electoral Code.
[197] OSCE/ODIHR Election Observation Report on Ukrainian 2012 Parliamentary Elections, pp. 2, 16, 18.

required by law.[198] As an observation, best practices of internal party democracy do require a plurality of choice, with at least two candidates competing for the nomination. The Slovenian Administrative Court[199] put aside the MEC's decision for rejection of the candidates' list on the basis of review of the internal procedures of the political party. The Administrative Court confirmed that the law imposes a requirement on the political parties to establish and abide by their rules for nominating candidates, along with the secrecy of vote and the residence requirement. It found that the MEC exceeded its competence, as the requirements of the MEC in that particular case were not the ones set out in the law. This case not only clarified the competencies of the MEC when reviewing internal party rules, but it also established clear limits on the MEC's actions in this regard.

- While the *principles of non-discrimination and equal treatment* are a shared value among all examined states, their translation into concrete terms does not come easy. For example, the UK is leading the way to ensure equal conditions for full enjoyment of the passive election right by the persons with disabilities, in order to increase their number in the representative bodies. See also *Mathieu-Mohin & Clerfayt v. Belgium*, where taking an oath in a particular language was made a criteria for taking an office.

Electoral Administration: -In the examined countries, *EMBs* fall broadly within three categories, as follows: a) the ex-socialist countries from the sample plus the UK[200] prefer the independent model, b) Belgium and Switzerland prefer the governmental model, and c) France uses a mixed model of the electoral administration.[201] In Macedonia, the composition of the State Electoral Commission, whereby only the biggest political parties can nominate candidates for members, sometimes drives the latter to vote along party lines[202] and leaves smaller parties without effective protection of their interests. In 2007, the Slovenian Constitutional Court decided that the Law on Local Elections was incompatible with the Constitution, as it had not outlawed the conflict of interest between being an EB member and being a candidate's close relative, which created nepotism.

---

[198] Grad, Svete, Lumbar, Predpise o Volitvah v Drzavni Zbor 2008 (2008) p. 56.
[199] Judgment no. U. 399/2008.
[200] GRECO, Third Evaluation Round, Evaluation Report on UK on Transparency of Party Funding (2007) p. 19.
[201] Data taken from Idea International at <http://www.idea.int> accessed on 6 July 2013.
[202] Siljanovska-Davkova, Ullom, Kranli, Skoric, Komentar na Izborniot Zakonik (2009) pp. 72-73 at<http://www.most.org.mk>.

IV. European Election Standards in National Jurisdictions: A Comparison

As a rule, all countries in their legislation foresee a certain level of transparency in the work of the electoral administration. As to the implementation of the transparency principle, according to ODIHR, in Ukraine the electoral administration should put more effort into opening its decision-making to the public, in order to strengthen public confidence and trust. As a confidence strengthening measure, in Macedonia the minutes from the counting and tallying of the results is made available to the public.

Equitable gender representation is one of the desiderata in line with the requirement to allow a greater access to public offices to women. Slovenia does not foresee a gender requirement for the composition of the EMBs, unlike Macedonia.

Electoral campaign: -The indispensable segments of the *electoral campaigning* for each candidate encompass: a) access to impartial media and b) the right to hold a rally. On the first segment, all the countries foresee free time for political presentation on the public broadcaster, along with paid political propaganda. Switzerland and Belgium prohibit paid political advertising on electronic media in line with the equal opportunity principle. Information about the parties' political programmes is conveyed via public radio and TV broadcast, as well as through print media.[203] As a comment, whereas such a prohibition might be seen as useful in other countries, it will only contribute to free and fair elections, if the public broadcaster ensures balanced and unbiased coverage. Otherwise, it might have an adverse effect on the freedom of expression, if the ruling party is "ruling" the public broadcaster.

In the UK, free time is allocated by electronic public and private media under equitable and fair conditions. Other indirect funding includes free postage to each voter and a use of meeting rooms free. Indirect funding is also available in Ukraine in a form of free air time, publication of election programmes and publication of candidates' lists.[204]

The enforcement of the above rights is not an easy task. In Macedonia, the "equal media access approach" applies. Whereas the Broadcasting Council monitors broadcasters, the print media and internet remain without a watchdog. Even the civil organizations committed to

---

[203] OSCE/ODIHR, Election Assessment Reports on Swiss 2011 Federal Elections and Belgian 2007 Parliamentary Elections.
[204] GRECO, Third Evaluation Round, Evaluation Reports on Transparency of Party Funding on UK (2007) pp. 7-8, and on Ukraine (2011) p. 8.

"free and fair elections" have not shown any interest in their monitoring. In Slovenia, neither the Court of Audit nor the Media or Market Inspectorates[205] are equipped for media monitoring. The civil sector also does not monitor the media. So, it is difficult to establish a violation committed by the media in this regard. However, nothing is preventing the political parties from being proactive, e.g., by performing their own media monitoring and reporting the violations to the authorities. The Ukrainian Law on Elections regulates the electoral campaign violations in detail and foresees broad sanctioning, i.e., a suspension of a licence and a temporary ban on publication.

The second important segment refers to the right to hold a rally within the electoral campaign framework. There are legal guarantees for the enjoyment of this right in all eight countries. However, on one hand the candidates sometimes struggle with undue interference with this right, e.g., in Azerbaijan and Ukraine. On the other hand, as a simplified example, the organizers of the electoral rally may be punished for a misdemeanour in Slovenia and Macedonia in the absence of prior notification.

Electoral campaign financing: -*Public funds* are disbursed to the candidates under the principles of equality or proportionality and non-discrimination. In Slovenia[206], the Constitutional Court abrogated a provision restricting direct public funding only to those parties that won mandates in the National Assembly. The Court opined that the provision was discriminatory. In addition, there was no proper justification for such a difference in the treatment of various political parties in view of the equality of election rights. It ordered the legislature to amend the provision to the effect that all parties reaching a certain threshold receive public funding. In the context of the need to have short deadlines when elections are tackled, the Constitutional Court took 2 years and 4 months to decide on the request submitted in 1996. Whether such a length of time was reasonable should be assessed from the viewpoint of whether or not there were elections in the meanwhile, as such a delay might have curtailed some parties' funds.

- An explicit *limit on donations* is perceived as a vital safeguard of the electoral fairness, since it is prescribed in all eight countries. The ceilings vary from country to country in terms

---

[205] OSCE/ODIHR Election Assessment Report on Slovenian 2011 National Assembly Elections, p. 16.
[206] Uradni List RS, no. 24/1999.

of the donors' category and of the value of the donation. The UK regulates also the upper limit of the expenditure made by third parties with the electoral campaign framework.[207]

The Macedonian experience shows that the amount of the donation made by natural persons is fixed, whereas the amount of the donations made by legal persons is flexible, depending on their annual turnover.[208] The upper admissible limit encompasses in-kind and money donations. In the UK, a free supply of venue and equipment is considered an in-kind contribution.[209]

- A prohibition of donations made by *corporations*, should be followed as it denotes best practice in the electoral campaign affairs. Such an example is French and Belgian legislation. The latter, however, allows sponsorships. Azerbaijan proscribes donations made by corporations only to the political parties, but not to the candidates, whereas for Ukraine it is *vice versa*.[210] Switzerland follows its liberal policies in relation to the electoral campaign financing and allows donations to be made by corporations with the state's ownership or holding a public contract.

- An electoral campaign can be *funded* by party fees, provided that a reporting requirement is observed. In particular, political parties' membership fees are among the legal sources of funding in the UK, Macedonia and France. They fall under the same regime for the limitation of the amounts of donations and for reporting of the incomes.

- Belgium, the United Kingdom, Slovenia and one of the Swiss cantons foresee specific limits on *anonymous donations*. The remainder of the countries prohibit anonymous donations, along with another Swiss canton. It appears that the rest of the Swiss cantons and the confederation do not have legislation in place in this regard.[211] As for France, there is no requirement for public disclosure to third parties of the donations not exceeding 3,000 Euro, which made donations insufficiently transparent.

---

[207] GRECO, Fighting Corruption Political Funding, Thematic Review of GRECO's Third Evaluation Round, p. 26 (...).
[208] Article 83 of the Electoral Code.
[209] GRECO, Fighting Corruption Political Funding, Thematic Review of GRECO's Third Evaluation Round, p. 12 (...).
[210] Idea International at <www.idea.int/uid/countryview.cfm?id=53> accessed on 6 July 2013.
[211] GRECO Evaluation Reports, Third Evaluation Round for all eight countries from the sample.

- Except for Belgium and Switzerland, the remainder of the subjects of the examination unanimously prohibits *foreign donations*. Judging according to GRECO findings, exceptions to this rule exist in the UK for small-scale specified expenditures, as well as in France for contributions from foreign individuals.

- The number of the registered voters serves as a perimeter for *limiting the electoral expenses*. France foresees strict penalties when more funds are disbursed than the legal maximum. The foreseen penalties include a fine, stripping the winning candidate off his mandate, a loss of the right to be reimbursed, and a payment of the exceeded amount to the public treasury. Also in Slovenia, when the limits for the allowed electoral spending are exceeded, the partial reimbursement of the costs and public funding is reduced or lost in accordance with the law. The above examples should be copied by other countries, as the loss of funds is a more effective deterrent then payment of fines. Political parties might prefer to pay a small fine, instead of ceasing the unlawful conduct, if breaking a law means increased chances to win elections.

- Whereas in Macedonia no expenditure is allowed outside of the *organized electoral campaign*, the Azerbaijani Electoral Code imposes normative standards on pre-electoral campaign activities. In the UK, Macedonia, Slovenia and France the inflow of cash and expenditure passes through an election agent. In the UK, third parties organizing campaign activities for an electoral candidate must register with the electoral commission and must abide by the rules imposing a ceiling on their expenditure.[212] Other countries, like Ukraine leave financing of the entities related to a political party unregulated, thus opening up a space for illegal campaign funding.[213]

- The *financial reporting* in the UK serves as a good example of accountability for electoral campaign financing. In particular, reporting is done on quarterly basis, with an increased frequency (once per week) during the election period. Loans are also reported, except by the election candidates who report separately on other types of received incomes. Multiple donations coming from the same source must be reported, if their aggregated sum is above the amount for which no reporting is required according to GRECO. The monitoring of

---

[212] GRECO, Third Evaluation Round, Evaluation report on UK on Transparency of Party Funding (2007) pp. 4, 11.
[213] OSCE/ODIHR Election Observation Report on Ukrainian 2012 Parliamentary Elections, p. 18.

electoral expenses is done by the Electoral Commission, which is in possession of investigative powers and access to documents.

Macedonia has also adopted the practice of multiple reporting. However, the length of the electoral campaign is only twenty days. This represents a major drawback with respect to freedom of expression, in light of the prohibition on campaigning outside of the electoral campaign period. The issue is connected with electoral campaign financing, since it is considered that there is a relationship between the length of the electoral campaign and the illegal practices. The concern that a longer campaign allows more time for illegal practices to occur cannot be accepted in light of its disproportionality to the principle of informed voters. Rather, other effective measures should be taken into account, like a prohibition of commercial advertisements in the media. In France, there is no continuous reporting during electoral campaign, but the electoral campaign reports must be submitted within 2 months of the elections, which was judged both by the OSCE/ODIHR and by GRECO as not in compliance with European standards. The Swiss federation should also improve the transparency of their electoral campaign financing.[214]

Legal remedies: - In some countries, legal standing to *challenge the composition of the candidates' lists* is restricted to their submitters and candidates. For instance, the Slovenian Constitutional Court examined who has the right to file an appeal with the Constitutional Court regarding confirmation of the MPs' mandates by the National Assembly.[215] The applicants, who apparently did not meet the threshold to be elected in their constituencies, complained that the national list of the party was not composed in accordance with the law. The Constitutional Court refused to examine the appeal on the merits, considering that only candidates and candidates' lists' representatives have the right to appeal as they were protecting their own rights. However, a separate opinion questioned the protection of the active election right of voters. It considered that the current right to appeal, given only to the candidates and candidate lists' representatives, did not afford effective protection to the voter. However, due care had to be given to avoid parallel protection systems, resulting in conflicting decisions. The particularity of Belgium regarding the candidates' lists' legal avenue, is the possibility to challenge the declaration of the linguistic belonging

---

[214] OSCE/ODIHR, Election Assessment Report on Swiss 2011 Federal Assembly Elections p. 9.
[215] Mp – 1/96.

with the Conseil d'état, whereas for the ineligibility issues the appeal should be filed with the appeals court.

Election observation: -Countries differ in law and practice in this regard, depending on their position on the democracy scale. Whereas developing democracies from the sample usually have legal provisions detailing *election observation*, in practice electoral observers face obstacles and a lack of access. For the old democracies plus Slovenia, a lack of provisions on electoral observation does not impede effective access to the electoral processes. The frequency of international election observations differs. For comparison, in Macedonia, all elections are subject to OSCE/ODIHR scrutiny (since 1996), while in Slovenia OSCE/ODIHR election observation is a recent trend.

Election Day

Voting: -Countries with a democratic tradition foresee *postal and proxy voting*, as yet another way to provide universal access to balloting. On balance, important safeguards must be in place to protect electoral integrity. By contrast, in Azerbaijan, Ukraine and Macedonia voters can cast their ballot only in person.

-The legal requirement for a *secret and free vote* is transcendent of the countries' boundaries. The subjects of examination converge on the point of the vote buying prohibition, which aims at protecting the free expression standard of the voters.

-As to the *voting instructions* in the minority languages, Ukrainian legislation seems restrictive, as Ukrainian is the sole language in which electoral materials may appear. However, such a prohibition proved difficult to defend in practice.[216]

-As a rule, *visually impaired persons* are assisted by another person in order to cast their vote. The OSCE/ODIHR recommended to France to look closely into the matter in order to protect their right to a secret vote.[217] For example, in Ukraine in each polling station there are available ballot stencils for this purpose.[218]

---

[216] OSCE/ODIHR Election Observation Report on Ukrainian 2012 Parliamentary Elections, p. 23.
[217] OSCE/ODIHR, Election Assessment Report on French 2012 Parliamentary Elections, p. 2.
[218] Ukrainian Law on Election of the Peoples' Deputies (2011) Article 85 (6).

IV. European Election Standards in National Jurisdictions: A Comparison

With respect to giving voters a fair chance to cast their vote, the legal solution of the Azerbaijani Code (Article 35, paragraph 3.1) which foresees polling stations with 1,500 voters does not seem to give a realistic opportunity to the voters to cast their vote.

Intimidation: -*Intimidation of voters* before and during election day was recorded as a problem in the 2008 and 2009 elections in Macedonia. Although ODIHR and local election observers received a considerable number of credible allegations of intimidation during the 2009 elections, the authorities asserted that no complaint was registered with the state bodies. However, when looking at the substance of the complaints submitted to the SEC by the candidates, a number of them allege intimidation of voters. Since the SEC rejected a majority of the complaints, it could be accepted that in such cases no irregularities occurred, provided that the complaints were thoroughly examined. Still, in the few cases where the SEC granted the complaint, it failed to ensure proper follow-up in terms of initiating criminal or misdemeanor proceedings, despite its legal obligation to report crimes.[219]

Technical novelties:- While, among others, France uses *e-voting*, ODIHR requires these systems to be publicly procured and reliable, the voters to be educated for its use and to have a possibility to make corrections.

Security: -As to *the security* during Election Day in Macedonia, the police has an obligation to maintain peace and order but only from a certain distance from the polling station. It can only enter and intervene when called by the electoral board in case of disorder or violence.[220] Similarly, in Belgium the president of an electoral board can ask for police assistance to restore peace and order in a polling station.[221]

- In France, the Constitutional Council *monitors the voting* in the polling stations to check the regularity of the process.[222] In Macedonia, it is the state electoral commission that monitors the voting procedures in the polling stations and can terminate the voting in case of gross irregularities.[223]

---

[219] OSCE/ODIHR Election Observation Reports on Macedonian 2008 Local and 2009 Parliamentary elections.
[220] Macedonian Electoral Code, Article 102.
[221] Belgian Electoral Code, Article 109.
[222] See information about the constitutional council at
<http//:127.0.0.180/conseil_conseil/root/core/d0001/04965>.
[223] Macedonian Electoral Code.

IV. European Election Standards in National Jurisdictions: A Comparison

<u>Counting</u>: In Macedonia, a criminal offence entitled electoral deceit prohibits election officials from changing the number of votes cast for the candidates, from manipulating the numbers during *counting* and tallying and from reporting fake election results. In Azerbaijan, significant problems were spotted during the counting of the votes, such as a presence of unauthorized persons during counting, a lack of legally prescribed reconciliation and interference with the process.[224] Counting of the votes in Slovenia posed a problem in 1997, because of the short deadlines for receiving the ballots. Upon a Constitutional Court's decision, the deadline within which the ballots received by mail were counted, was prolonged in order to include as many votes in the counting as possible. In UK, ODIHR recommended the allocation of voters and polling station members to be measured in proportion to the needs to enable all voters to cast their votes.

Post-election Period

<u>Electoral results:</u> *Tallying* of the results must be a transparent process in order to inspire public confidence in the winner of the electoral competition. However, in Azerbaijan, the transparency requirement was not fully observed during the tabulation of the 2008 electoral results.[225] Belgium in 2007 encountered a different, but not insignificant problem during the tabulation due to a breakdown of the electronic equipment.

<u>Audit</u>: -In Ukraine and the UK, the *oversight of the electoral campaign funding* is done by the main electoral commission, receiving reports about the sources, types and value of the incomes and expenditures. In Macedonia, the oversight task is allocated to the State Audit Office. Reckoning that its competence by law is only limited to auditing of public funds, the State Audit Office does not audit the expenditures made from private funds, despite the public interest involved. In fact, this means that independent candidates' expenditures are never audited, since they do not receive public funds. On balance, the reports are subject to public disclosure and are also received by the State electoral commission and the anti-corruption commission. In addition, the State Audit Office only audits the biggest parties' electoral campaign expenditures in accordance with its annual plan, due to the shortage of resources and funds. Slovenia has solved this problem by giving its Audit Court competence

---

[224] OSCE/ODIHR Election Observation Report on Azerbaijani 2010 Parliamentary Elections, p. 20.
[225] OSCE/ODIHR Election Observation Report on Azerbaijani 2008 Presidential Elections, p. 24.

also to audit subjects that do not receive public funds, thus protecting the public interest in free and fair elections, as well as the rights of others.

Legal remedies: -Various *corrective justice measures* are at the disposal of the countries, with various arbiters ranging from electoral commissions to courts. As to the electoral disputes in France, the Constitutional Council deals only with complaints relating to general elections, whereas the remainder of election-related complaints are processed by the administrative courts.[226] The administrative court, along with the state electoral commission, represents the forum for the resolution of electoral disputes in Macedonia. The deadlines within which these adjudicative bodies must adopt a decision are among the shortest ones in comparison to other countries from the sample. Short deadlines coupled with a huge number of objections[227] and lawsuits, substantially weaken the effectiveness of the electoral disputes' for the sake of the efficiency requirement. In order to reconcile efficiency with effectiveness, Macedonia could look into the possibility of introducing mediation as a way to resolve electoral disputes. As a good example, in Switzerland, a majority of the electoral disputes are resolved even before reaching the court, which contributes to the efficiency of the system. In Macedonia, public hearings are statutory requirement, dissimilar to Slovenia.

- A *challenge to election results* is granted to diverse stakeholders, ranging from political party representatives and candidates to registered voters.[228] France has the most "generous" solution in this regard, as the voters have also the right to challenge the validity of elections. A similar legal solution has been accepted in Ukraine, since an election observer may also challenge the electoral result. The downside of such a solution is when election observers are denied access. Furthermore, the issue of a conflict with the observers' impartiality may arise, especially when there is a "hidden" connection with some of the electoral candidates. Finally, the observers might not be equipped to start legal proceedings, thus legal protection for a lawful elections, should be shared among a diversified portfolio of stakeholders.

-As a rule, the prerogative to *annul an election result* or a part of it rests with the court. In Macedonia and Azerbaijan, such power is also vested in the highest electoral administrative

---

[226] Idea International , Electoral Justice Handbook (2010), pp. 128-129 at <http://www.idea.int>.
[227] For example, in the 2009 elections, the SEC received 98 objections only in the first round.
[228] See the database on electoral justice at <www.idea.int>.

body.[229] In the latter country, the court and the central election commission have concurrent jurisdiction, which might result in contradictory decisions. Furthermore, the grounds for annulling the results are drafted in broad terms, which is contrary to the requirement of legal certainty and consistency. Evenmore so, irregularities benefiting a losing candidate are not foreseen as a ground to cancel elections. This is a broadly drafted provision, prone to abuse, as it fails to take into consideration the consequences that such irregularities bear on other "losers" of the election. By contrast, the Macedonian law stipulates an annulment of elections in a polling station in the case of established irregularities, which serves as a remedy. However, the voting can only be repeated when election results are affected. Such a stipulation effectively disenfranchises the voters and takes away the possibility of the political parties to obtain a refund from public funds, if the election is not repeated. Elections are repeated when irregularities have been discovered that affect the election result. By contrast, in Slovenia, if irregularities are discovered which do not affect the election result, the elections are not annulled. In France, a complaint with no effect on election results can be rejected, but the rejection must be justified.[230] Nonetheless, when there is no annulment, the irregularities committed remain unsanctioned unless other types of legal remedies are pursued. In addition, it is unclear how those votes are counted in order to receive public funds.

-Acknowledging the fact that no *sanctions* were ever imposed in Ukraine until 2011, it follows that the authorities have not effectively used the means at their disposal to combat impunity in the electoral financing realm.[231] In UK, more flexible sanctions have been introduced by way of secondary legislation. While the use of secondary legislation as an instrument of punishment may be more efficient, it may not be acceptable to other countries, which may consider the Parliament a better-suited forum to determine sanctions especially in the electoral campaign realm.

Remedies for breach of the electoral financing rules are well-developed in France, and include a loss of public funds, fines, a loss of exemption from supervision by the Audit Court and imprisonment. From the statistics presented in the GRECO report, until 2009 there were not a significant number of cases in quantitative terms, relating to electoral campaign

---

[229] Azerbaijani Electoral Code, Article 114.
[230] French Electoral Code, LO 183.
[231] GRECO, Third Evaluation Round, Evaluation Report on Ukraine on Transparency of Party Funding (2011) pp. 18-19.

violations. However, some of the cases including the recent ones, involve the decision-makers, former French presidents, indicating the resolve of judicial authorities to protect the paradigm of "free and fair elections" from corrupt practices.

In Slovenia, there is a lenient sentencing policy. Such a policy might ensue from a low rate of election-related criminality. In particular, only in one case was a person convicted for having committed a crime against voting rights and elections in 2008, whereas there were no convictions in 1995, 2000 and 2004 – 2007. According to the 2002 crime statistics, there were only a few cases of criminal investigations, which appeared to be low-profile. In particular, there were 7 cases in total, in connection with the right to vote and elections, out of which 1 concerned a violation of the free choice of voters and the remainder referred to the destruction, or forgery of election documents. Only in the case connected with the violation of the free choice of voters was the complaint rejected and in the rest of the cases, the perpetrators were not discovered. Regarding the trial stage in 2002, there were four indictments for a violation of the right to vote. In all four cases the indictments were rejected and the procedures stopped.[232] The above statistical information may also indicate a lack of effective investigation on the part of the authorities, taking into consideration that election irregularities did occur, as it is shown in the part devoted to electoral disputes. Moreover, in case of irregularities, the EMB members have a statutory obligation to report criminal behavior to the prosecution. The above statement about the possible lack of effective investigation is further supported by the fact that between 1998 and 2004 only 1 out of 14 requests for misdemeanors filed by the Court of Audit was processed. The rest were declared inadmissible mainly because the statute of limitations had expired.[233] Slovenia might wish to reconsider its approach towards prosecutorial and sentencing policy in relation to elections with the aim of preventing and effectively deterring election-related offences.

As a rule, if a country has legislation regulating presidential pardon or amnesty, the electoral offences are not excluded from the general regime.

- Office occupied by the winning candidate: A positive example comes from Belgium, which requires a *wholesome*, balanced and honest approach from the elected representatives to their constituencies and not only to the voters who voted for them.[234]

---

[232] Statistical Office of the Republic of Slovenia (2005).
[233] GRECO Eval III Rep (2009) 6E, Theme II (2007) p. 22.
[234] Belgian Constitution, Article 42.

IV. European Election Standards in National Jurisdictions: A Comparison

As a bottom-line, the results of the examination of the national electoral legislation and its implementation through the prism of the evolved European standards demonstrate that no country is immune from the problems in electoral realm. As a result, the assumption that consolidated democracies from the sample have no concerns with respect to electoral democracy is replaced with the assumption that consolidated democracies have fewer worries with electoral democracy in comparison to democracies in development. Indeed, it was shown that the EU member states from the sample struggle with electoral campaign financing, low turnout of voters and the universality of the vote. Democracies that are in the process of consolidation, still face problems that speak to the fundaments of democracy, such as arbitrary limitations of freedoms of association and expression, of freedom of movement and continuing to mix the ruling parties with the state.

For further analysis, the countries are divided into four groupings on the basis of their similarities and common challenges. The first grouping covers all eight countries. In view of the afore-mentioned assumption, the work shows that despite differences among the compared countries, they all face common problems at a systematic level. The common challenge, primarily, refers to electoral campaign financing and its various segments, including lawful sources, reporting, monitoring, transparency and auditing. Another common challenge refers to sustainable electoral participation of minorities and women, which seems to meet some reluctance from the established political elites, as it shapes the societies within. In fact, greater inclusion of minorities and women in public affairs is a question of democratic culture, and not of rules and regulations. It is recommended for the countries that have not done so, to lower the voting age and allow 16 years old to vote, in order to get used to democracy from a young age. Further recommendation across the groupings is to prohibit donations from corporations in order to reduce oligarchic influence in politics.

The second selected grouping of countries includes only the EU member states. The common challenge is embodied in a low voter turnout in the European elections, which in substance symbolizes low interest in European affairs. A lack of provisions regulating election observation is yet another shared feature.

For the selected grouping of democracies in consolidation inclusive and participatory law-making represents one of the main challenges in the electoral arena. Accurate and updated voters' lists, along with an abuse of administrative resources during the time of elections, belong also to the group of common problems, which these countries need to resolve. On a separate note, Ukraine and Azerbaijan, as a sub-grouping of countries that do not geographically belong to Europe, struggle to protect and maintain a meaningful opposition, and fail to protect the right of the opposition to hold a rally.

Switzerland as a model democracy, but a non-EU member state, stands alone in this exercise. The examination shows a surprising result regarding its federal elections that appear to be under-regulated and mostly driven by separate cantonal rules. Such a result may highlight the value of a long-standing electoral practice, which does not necessitate strict laws or sanctions to be self-perpetuating, for it has become a part of the political culture of the country. Nevertheless, the Swiss Federation needs to address certain shortcomings regarding electoral campaigning for federal elections. In particular, it should look at prohibiting certain types of donations in accordance with European standards. Prohibition of foreign and anonymous donations will enhance electoral campaign transparency, while interdiction of receiving donations from public or publicly contracted companies will prevent corruption. Finally, for greater promotion of the universality of election rights, the Swiss Federation should invest greater effort into inclusion of persons with disabilities as electoral candidates with a real prospect of being elected.

From the individual examination of the remainder of the countries from the selected sample, the following is observed:

Azerbaijan, figuratively speaking, needs to fight the "free and fair elections" battle on several battlefields. First, it should strive for more inclusive and transparent law-making in the electoral arena, without including too much detail in the law that can otherwise be put in secondary legislation. Second, it should increase the effectiveness of its justice system and clarify the role of the prosecutor who seems to be taking over the role of the courts regarding hypothetical incarcerations of electoral candidates. Third, it should put in place specific measures for increased participation of women and minorities in public affairs. Fourth, freedom of peaceful assembly must also be protected for the opposition, and not only for the ruling party. Fifth, PSs should be re- fashioned in accordance with the realistic number of voters per PS. Sixth, transparency of counting and tallying procedures should be enhanced to increase public confidence in election results. Finally, it should introduce continuous education for voters.

IV. European Election Standards in National Jurisdictions: A Comparison

Next country in alphabetical order, Belgium has also certain electoral desiderata to fulfil. For example, it should cut the sub-national electoral mandates that are longer than five years in order to avoid concentration of power in hands of the elites, as well as for renewed legitimacy of the decision-making bodies. It should further prohibit foreign donations, which might influence the course of domestic politics to detriment of eligible voters. It should also ensure that the e-voting is done in line with the applicable European election standards.

France should also consider shortening the mandates of elected sub-national bodies to five instead of six years for the same reasons as above. It should also improve its electoral campaign reporting to re-gain transparency and prevent corruption. France should also improve secrecy of the vote for blind persons by foreseeing ballot stencils for the blind.

A number of substantial electoral changes should be introduced by Macedonian authorities regarding several electoral variables, in line with European standards. Regarding legislative variables, modifications to election legislation (also when initiated by international factor) should not be seen as a possibility for introducing provisions that are inconsistent with the "free and fair elections" standard. Regarding the electoral eligibility variable, Macedonia should look into the possibility to extend election rights for local elections to non-nationals and stateless persons, in order to get their commitment and involvement in communal interest. Furthermore, it must also ensure the equality of vote in diaspora voting, unless it has a proper justification why the voters from the diaspora are in a more privileged position than the rest of the voters. It should also consider including a requirement for continuous education of voters, e.g., through citizens' schools of democracy. Furthermore, there must be put in place an adequate protection of voters from threats and intimidations. Last but not least, Macedonia should foresee ballot stencils for blind voters. Regarding electoral campaign variable, a clear separation between party and administrative resources must be maintained. Authorities may also wish to extend the period for the electoral campaign to enable better information for the voters. While a shorter electoral campaign is beneficial in cases when public order and safety might be jeopardized during the election period, Macedonia is no longer in such a phase, judging by its past elections. As for the electoral campaign financing, there must be an effective impartial audit of the funds of the candidates and political parties coming from private sources. Flexible donations from companies should not be allowed. The EMBs variable requires representativeness of smaller parties in order to satisfy the fairness principle. The country may also look into the possibility of systematic inclusion of the minority communities in the EMBs. Finally, the adequate remedy variable requires a repetition of the vote whenever elections are annulled, even when the electoral outcome has not been affected. A lack of re-run might make sense when there are security threats, but in Macedonia that is no longer a case. A lack of re-run not only deprives voters of their right to effectively cast their vote, but also deprives the candidates from obtaining an accurate picture about the number of votes won in the elections, and has its repercussions on the public funds received.

While Slovenia should be commended for its efforts to promote internal party democracy, the law should require at least two competing candidates for the primaries. Further possibilities for improvement encompass a reserved seat for Roma at the national level, on equal terms with the rest of the minority communities; and a requirement for equitable representation of women in EMBs (including at the highest level). Slovenia must improve its media monitoring, thus curbing impunity in this area. Greater inclusion of the civil sector in electoral law-making is also desirable with the aim of properly addressing their concerns and dwelling on their proposals.

The UK should also address a number of electoral concerns. It should strive to individualize circumstances under which prisoners could or could not vote, instead of opting for a blanket prohibition. Prohibition of voting for persons who went bankrupt should be abolished. The UK should also prohibit donations from public companies or companies holding a public contract and should make more realistic estimations about the number of voters per PS.

The last country, Ukraine should introduce a number of improvements in the legislative arena. First, it should improve transparency in its electoral law-making process, and should avoid including too many details in the laws, thus making them inflexible. Second, it should look into possibilities for making stateless persons and non-nationals eligible in line with the universality principle. Third, the authorities need better implementation of the equality principle when drawing electoral boundaries. Fourth, separation of powers must be strictly guarded during the electoral campaign in order to satisfy the fairness principle. For the same reason, a transparent decision-making of its EMBs must be fully preserved as the fifth recommendation. Sixth, candidates should not be required to satisfy a five-year residence requirement and must have their right to rally protected in order to safeguard the plurality of elections. Seventh, there must be voting instructions in the minority language to satisfy the "informed voter requirement".

IV. European Election Standards in National Jurisdictions: A Comparison

The summed-up results based on the interface of the two variables used, i.e., the national legislation and the evolved European election standards suggest that there is a high convergence among the states relating to the electoral principles *in abstracto*. On their application *in concreto* the convergence is higher among the states belonging to the same category. Similarly, the problems are also shared among the states from the same category. The importance of the number of adopted rules and regulations decreases with an increase of the acceptance of the democratic electoral culture.

The results of the above exercise, demonstrating that all examined countries struggle with a certain electoral segment, do not disprove the theory that national election standards can serve as a source of European election standards. The reasons are as follows:

Firstly, the exercise identified a high level of convergence among the states regarding the constituent elements of the "free and fair" electoral paradigm. A majority of the examined states use similar qualifications for the enjoyment of the electoral rights, although some of them differ regarding their limitation. Furthermore, they converge on the points of the upper value of the electoral threshold, on the electoral interval of parliamentary elections, on voters' education, on creating equal electoral conditions for disabled, on the incompatibility of functions with certain nuances, on audit and on corrective justice measures.

Secondly, some of the states show progressive rules and practices in certain electoral areas. For instance, the UK is leading the way to ensure equal conditions for full enjoyment of the passive election right by the persons with disabilities, in order to increase their number in the representative bodies. A further positive example comes from Azerbaijan that includes stateless persons in a different category than foreign nationals, and grants them wider election rights. The electors in consolidated democracies traditionally enjoy high confidence due to respect for the rule of law principle. The positive examples may be shared with other states wanting to enhance their electoral democracy, thus inspiring them to accept new European election standards.

Thirdly, elections are held by the states and not by the inter-governmental organizations. It is the states that are electoral units and not the organizations. If the European standards are developed only vertically by the international actors, such a process will divorce theory from practice with all negative ramifications. Fourthly, national legislation provides a wealth of concrete measures (or electoral interpretive standards) about the enforcement of the paradigm of "free and fair elections".

Lastly, elections are not frozen unchangeable matter. On the contrary, they constantly develop through the practice of democracy and ever-changing technological progress. Therefore, rules and practices of the most progressive states in this regard, could be used as an indicator of the electoral progress in the "post-communist" era.

It follows that the European election standards will be impoverished and could not keep pace with electoral developments if there was no constant exchange between the international and the national level.

V. NEVER-ENDING DEBATE: CONCLUSIONS AND RECOMMENDATIONS

Commitment to Free and Fair Elections

The ideological dimension of international law rests on the democratic principles, respect for human rights and justice in view of its correlation with the worldwide peace.[235] The people's right to participate in elections lies at the heart of contemporary democracy. The fact remains that the guarantees for "free and fair elections" vary depending on the cultural, political, historical and economic dimensions. However, election rights that are minimal, vaguely defined and not enforceable do not serve the purpose of democracy. Holding of elections cannot be considered sufficient for a society to be considered democratic, as it could lead to a sustainable survival of competitive authoritarianisms[236], especially when the connected political rights are not sufficiently protected.

European perspective

Within the context of regional electoral protection, the election standards in Europe remain a controversial topic for examination and subject to many constraints. In particular, there is vast and inaccessible data, a divergence among the states in terms of legal, political and social culture, subjectivity in interpreting international standards, internal cultures of the examined international/regional organizations, the sovereign rights of the states, the plurality of democratic theories. While acknowledging the above constraints, the examination clearly indicates that the solutions offered by the international dimension only partially respond to the needs of the praxis, as the citizens are still unable in many European countries to freely cast their vote or stand for elections. The problem is a multidimensional one even when only external factors are examined. The realist approach requires the discussion relating to the European standards in elections be expended on the following three dimensions:

The *first dimension* relates to whether or not these standards lack the required precision and legal force to be binding upon the states. The most important election standards for Europe are dispersed in the documents of the OSCE and CoE, organizations with a larger membership than the EU. Since the electoral principles enunciated by these organizations overlap, their reflection in the specific standards mirrors each other. All three organizations

---

[235] Kelly, Monitoring Democracy (2013) p. 26.
[236] Levitsky, Way, Autocracy by Democratic Rules: The Dynamics of Competitive Authoritarianism in the Post Cold War Era (rev. 2003) p. 7.

robustly safeguard the requirement of legality. While the OSCE uses the ECtHR judgments and the Code of Good Practice in Electoral Matters as an auxiliary source for the specific standards, the CoE electoral bodies benefit from the ODIHR's practical field experience with respect to electoral operations and procedures. The above "happy situation" resulting from a mutual recognition of the standards set by another organization is not compulsory, i.e., it has not become a norm. It rather comes in a sporadic way, on a case-by-case basis. Regarding the third organization of the electoral triumvirate -the EU, it is the only organization with all its members having a parallel membership in the CoE and the OSCE. It follows that only EU member states are bound by the electoral commitments originating from all three main sources at the European level.

Furthermore, the CoE and EU election standards are overwhelmingly conceptualized in terms of protection of individual human rights and liberties under the liberal democracy model. In the OSCE region, the onus is put on the states to organize elections in line with its commitments.

As to the content, if the legal hierarchy of the three sets of standards is ignored, the OSCE and CoE commitments may be perceived as duplication from their common member states' perspective. However, there is a difference between them, as it is only the CoE instruments that require free and fair elections for the local self-government units, even for non-citizens.[237] Furthermore, an explicit requirement for an impartial electoral administration is missing from the OSCE political commitments, although it is one of the major points of its electoral examination. On the other hand, it is only the OSCE commitments that require election observation scrutiny. Neither the OSCE nor the CoE consider a special type of electoral system as a vital precondition for "free and fair elections", dissimilar to the EU. The latter's valid election standards are contracted, and concentrate on the elections of its interest. As a ramification, in the EU there is a deepening and crystallization of the election standards, reflected to a specific electoral model (with a diapason of possibilities), an explicit upper limit of the electoral threshold and a prohibition on the accumulation of certain types of offices. The EU has also passed well-developed rules about electoral campaign funding from EU public funds. Whereas both the EU and the CoE have rules about the accumulation of functions, no such explicit rules exist in the OSCE region. For the CoE and the EU to grant election rights to non-nationals at the local level is not taboo. Finally, all three organizations

---

[237] The Charter of Local-Self Government and the Convention for the Participation of Foreigners in Public Life at Local Level.

rely on the generally permissible reasons for the limitation of the electoral rights, balanced under the principle of proportionality.

All three organizations use instruments of a different nature. Whereas the CoE has a combination of legally and non-legally-binding texts, the OSCE participating states are obliged to follow the politically-binding commitments. The EU, as a mixture of an inter-governmental and a supranational organization, varies in its approach and the policy regarding elections from the CoE and OSCE, in that its electoral pieces of legislation are legally-binding upon its members. Although the instruments are to some extent complementary, a combination of substance, a hierarchy of acts and mass electoral observations makes the OSCE political commitments more precise and demanding in practice when compared to the CoE legal norms. However, the only pan-European legally-binding provisions for legislative bodies and local self-government bodies are elaborated under the auspices of the CoE. In any case, no legally-binding document detailing the European election standards exists. The ECHR is only applied to the elections of a legislature. Even then, from the ECtHR case-law it is visible that the countries enjoy a wide margin of appreciation, which seems to confirm what has been put in the Code: the existence of different traditions when elections are at stake makes difficult application of common standards. Neither the ECHR, nor the Charter or other conventions herein provide more detail regarding common election standards. It is only the Code which offers more substance regarding the international election standards, and it is used as a comprehensive guideline for conducting elections. Nevertheless, the Code does not elaborate much about election campaign funding and media regulation. The CoE has already developed specific electoral campaign recommendations, with a follow-up procedure, dissimilar to the OSCE.

The issue of the lack of legally-binding precise election standards gains more importance in view of the fact that a number of the CoE and OSCE countries are already bound by a convention on election standards differing from the ones set out in the CoE documents. This issue has been also emphasized in the part devoted to the OSCE and has already caused problems in practice during election observation.

In view of the above, one cannot escape the impression that the picture relating to the European election standards is rather eclectic. In particular, there is no deepening of the election standards, but a proliferation of documents and declarations devoted to them. The greatest detail in this regard is offered by the election observation reports, guidelines, decisions, judgments and views of international bodies, but they either pertain to a particular country or to a case with its specific features, or have no binding force. As stated above, the ECtHR heavily relies on the margin of appreciation and the specific historical-political context when examining election-related cases. So, on one hand, objective standards can be found in the international documents, but they are not detailed enough. On the other hand, the more detailed explanations found in international decisions pertaining to individuals or countries are colored with the particular circumstances of the case. In spite of the proposals, ideas and demands for detailed election norms at the regional level, the existing commitments remain spread out in many texts. The question arises as to whether or not the current situation creates a patchwork, or an effective frame for conducting and assessing the elections?

The answer to the above question is that the general election principles and specific standards in Europe are set out in the documents with various legal value of the European electoral triumvirate. While reckoning the value of the above instruments for uncovering the European paradigm of "free and fair" elections, the objection that they lack detail and precision with respect to specific electoral topics is valid.

The practical problems stemming from the lack of precision and unequal legal force creates problems in using the international election observation as a tool to assess the integrity of elections. Election assessments have been seriously challenged by some states, mostly along west-east lines, because of electoral criteria not being clearly set out in the relevant reports. The recipient-state may also not put sufficient trust in the regional supervisory mechanism accusing it of the application of double standards, which as a ramification might have a loss of reputation for the international law subjects. Agreeing on precise and detailed election standards instead of offering three electoral nuances will help solve the above-mentioned inter-state problems.

The *second dimension* questions whether or not it is possible to define common election standards valid for all the states and European organizations and, if so, in which form. The fact remains that there are substantial economic cultural, historical and political differences between the states in Europe, in addition to the states' asymmetric powers. However, in comparison to the global level, the pro-regionalists' argument that the members of a regional organization can find a common ground easier because of their convergence in culture and tradition, should also be valid with respect to elections.

V. Neverending debate: conclusions and recommendations

In CoE and OSCE there is no willingness to accept such a convention. The reason asserted was that such a convention would lower the already existing standards. However, there is already a Convention on European standards ratified by the CIS countries, which are CoE and OSCE members. If the CIS countries have already been legally bound by a convention with lower election standards, what are the reasons for not accepting their proposal and elaborating a more detailed CoE convention, which would be up to present standards? Such a convention could be also used for effectively bridging the gap between the East and the West, which appears to be growing wider when elections are at stake. If the polarization on "Eastern European standards" and "Western European standards" continues, the electoral gap between the two groups of states may grow even wider, resulting in two separate standards of "free and fair elections" by function of geography and political culture. Such a situation risks rendering current sets of electoral standards of the CoE and OSCE ineffective for a considerable number of countries that are still in the process of democratic consolidation.

So, the issue that arises here is not whether or not a convention on European election standards is needed, but rather whether there is a political agreement among the CoE and OSCE states, as well as the EU to arrive at such a convention. It will only be useful if it sets out detailed election standards encompassing the existing CoE, OSCE, UN and possible EU standards, addressing the noticed re-occurring election irregularities and foreseeing an efficient supervisory mechanism, complementary to the existing ones. However, the fact remains that the European organizations vary in terms of their membership, goals and connectivity between their members. Election standards are seen by them through various prisms, i.e., of a deeper union, of a more secure Europe, or of a sustainable democracy and fully protected human rights.

One of the reasons asserted against the election standards' convention might be found in the states' sovereignty. The states, especially the powerful ones, might not be willing to be bound by detailed election norms, considering that such an instrument will interfere with their sovereignty.[238] Indeed, if there were to be negotiations for such a convention, a concerted effort of the states to lower the election standards, if legally-binding, should be expected. Such a hypothetical convention should not spell out only the major principles, if the aim is to provide added value. It should, actually go well deep in the issues like the funding of

---

[238] Steiner, Alston, International Human Rights in Context, Law, Politics, Morals (2nd edition) (2000) p. 572.

V. Neverending debate: conclusions and recommendations

financial campaign, anti-corruption measures, the freedom of the media, impartiality of the EMBs, plurality of choice and informed voters, election operations, counting and tabulation procedures, evidence and procedure for remedying electoral irregularities, criminal law elements against impunity and maybe even giving a framework for the political parties' and NGOs' conduct. If the hypothetical convention were only a shallow agreement, because it lacks precision and (as the case may be) enforcement measures, the only effect that it might produce would be to lower the existing standards. In conclusion, the argument against the election standards' convention is not based on an assumption that the present documents are sufficiently detailed and cover all the issues, since in many instances it is difficult to persuade the governments what are the applicable election standards regarding a specific issue. Rather, the argument against the election standards' convention is based on the nature of international law and its principles, as well as on the political argument based on the observation of the states' behavior, when elections are at stake. In addition, the issue is burdened with the east-west division and different political outlook.

The ratification of a treaty might be advantageous in case a state refuses to honor the existing commitments. Still, the current mix of legally and non-legally-binding standards, do influence the state behavior, although their influence might originate more from the world of politics than from the world of law. The existing mosaic of the election standards' pledges and norms at the international level do represent a solid legal framework in case there is firm political support to preserve the integrity of elections.

Taking into consideration that: 1) there are legally-binding election standards; 2) there are politically binding electoral commitments; 3) there is no shortage of electoral guidelines and recommendations; and 4) there is no momentum for negotiating a detailed legally-binding convention, the following is recommended:

First, in order to avoid a proliferation of documents in the electoral arena, which might add to more confusion, the common European election standards should take the legal form of a trilateral agreement for cooperation signed by the CoE, the OSCE and the EU. The agreement will unify and ensure coherence among the election standards of the three organizations, by providing an exhaustive list of concretely defined standards for each phase of the electoral cycle. It should be publicly promoted and made accessible in each of the states concerned. According to Kelly whereas there is a continuing debate about what a proper election means,

V. Neverending debate: conclusions and recommendations

at "operational level that is quite workable". Under this presumption, it will suffice to articulate at the international political level what the operational level has already established under the paradigm of "free and fair elections" in a legal form of an agreement.[239] Furthermore, since the members of the three European organizations have already agreed and subscribed to certain conduct in terms of elections, the European organizations should have a *de facto* mandate to conceptualize common election standards in the form of a trilateral agreement signed among the three European organizations. A legally-binding trilateral agreement will not only clearly define European standards in the election field, but it will also set out the responsibilities, goals and forms of cooperation between the signatories.

The above-mentioned agreement will need the approval of the decision-making bodies of the three organizations in line with their internal rules. Since a problem of approval might be encountered at this level, a memorandum of understanding can be used as an alternative. This "softer" legal instrument can be still used for articulating common European standards, which must be sufficiently precise and clear, in order to have any added value.

However, empirical evidence show that cooperation agreements regulating modalities of joint actions in the area of democratization and protection of human rights and rule of law have already been concluded in the past by the relevant international organizations.[240] Regarding the election arena, it is worth mentioning the recommendation to sign an agreement on election observation between CoE and OSCE.[241] Furthermore, judging by the mandates of the three international organizations, their member/participating states have expressed a clear intent for them to be involved in safeguarding free and fair elections in Europe. It is clear that on the substantive side, the agreement will undoubtedly further the above objective.

---

[239] Monitoring Democracy (2013) p. 26.
[240] For example: Cooperation agreement between European Community and CoE on cooperation between Agency of Fundamental Rights and CoE published in Official Journal of EU, I.186/7 (2008); 2005 Cooperation agreement between the Committee of Regions of EU and CLRAE (CoE), revised in 2009; Cooperation agreement signed between OSCE and CoE for building effective democracy and good governance at local and regional level in South-East Europe at : www.coe.int / www.coe.ge
http://www.coe.int/t/dgap/tbilisi/archives/enews/EEFkVlEkylxQSzLmPs.asp dated 30 august 2014; Cooperation agreement between the EU Commission and CoE on human rights, democracy and rule of law signed (press release dated 1 April 2014).
[241] Ulfstein, The CoE and the OSCE: Enhancing co-operation and complementarity through greater coherence, DPP (2012)1, p. 18 at<http://www. coe.int>.

V. Neverending debate: conclusions and recommendations

As to the power to conclude the agreement, OSCE and EU appear to be a more peculiar case in comparison to CoE[242]; with OSCE not having a constituent treaty and EU being in possession of supranational elements. For OSCE, the participating states' consent for cooperation with two other international organizations has been expressed, *inter alia*, in the 1999 Istanbul document in the part devoted to co-operation with other organizations: the platform for co-operative security and subsequent PC decisions.[243] For EU it is clear that it has both a mandate[244] and power to conclude international agreements, in the area of foreign policy, development and cooperation, which covers electoral support arena. As a rule, the above-mentioned agreement will be part of the EU legal order; a secondary source of law, and thus binding upon the EU institutions. However, its scope should be well-defined as electoral matters are also part of the internal power resting with the states.

An additional point that needs to be answered, relates to the legal nature of the trilateral agreement for cooperation and to its governing law. Without any doubt, the above international agreement will be a part of international legal order, with the general principles of law applicable. However, taking into consideration the signatories, the duty bearers, scope and the objective of the agreement, it appears that the agreement would have elements of the emerging concept of global administrative law, and thus its principles of transparency, accountability and rule of law should also govern the agreement.

When examining the effects of such an agreement with respect to member states[245], the focus is placed on EU. This agreement will not create direct rights of individuals and will not be enforceable in local courts. In particularly, while examining the conditions for direct effect of international agreements, it appears that its first condition, the provisions to be clear and precise enough, might be easily fulfilled. The second "unconditionallity" condition may be also fulfilled. However, the third condition, not requiring any further implementing measures, will not be fulfilled, as elections in the EU countries will continue to be governed by their respective electoral legislation, and not by the trilateral agreement. It is not and it cannot be the role of the agreement to substitute for national election legislation, and directly interfere with the electoral area, which is traditionally a prerogative of a sovereign state, especially

---

[242] For power to conclude a cooperation agreement, see also Articles 15 and 16 of the Statute of CoE.

[243] PC Journal no. 535, Decision no. 637 (2004) and PC Journal no. 553, Decision no. 670 (2005) on cooperation between OSCE and CoE.

[244] Article 220 of TFEU.

[245] Bogdandy, General Principles of International Public Authority: Sketching a Research Field , German Law Journal, Vol. 9, No. 1 (2008) pp. 1930-1931.

V. Neverending debate: conclusions and recommendations

when the states have not consented to it. However, the agreement in conjunction with other above-mentioned documents, which contain European electoral standards will indirectly create obligations for the states (of all three organizations) to bring their electoral legislation into compliance with the election standards stipulated in the agreement.[246]

Second, instead of focusing on an electoral convention, the European regional organizations should increase their focus on the inclusion of detailed provisions on various electoral topics in the member states' national laws, in line with the internationally recognized election standards. The richness of comparative systems provides an additional basis to achieve this objective and provides a justification for using the regional approach. Although it is not necessary to have a single system of election standards among the European organizations, their interpretation should be as consistent as possible. They should be widely disseminated not only to the political actors and state bodies, but also to the citizens. The second face of the god Janus, signals that the concerted advocacy effort might be undermined by a lack of resources and funds, lengthy and untimely procedures contributing to the loss of momentum, and a lack of opportunity for an effective follow-up in this regard. A lack of explicit mandate and the restraint coming from the principle of sovereignty of the states might also have a role to play in this regard. Recalling that the elections are a system of a vertical accountability to the citizens, respect for free and fair elections can only contribute to citizens' expression of sovereignty.

The *third dimension* points to the lacunae in the existing European election standards. There is an intention to improve and reform the existing OSCE, CoE and EU commitments, in a spirit of time, to keep abreast with the theoretical and technological electoral innovations (e-voting, internet) to the extent allowed by the political negotiations. In this endeavor, clear articulation of the standard of electoral outcome is missing. This standard is connected with the quality of the representative democracy. It is inconceivable that democracy will perpetuate itself indefinitely, or that it will be sustained by an invisible hand, in the absence of the pre-conditions for its very existence.

The pillars of the architecture of the meaningful representation standard have been already set in a theoretical thought and in the internationally recognized standards. According to

---

[246] Davies, Understanding European Union Law (2013) pp. 73-75.

V. Neverending debate: conclusions and recommendations

Lijphard, a low voter turnout signals political inequality and uninterested voters. The conversation should not be limited to informed and educated voters, but should open up to the quality of the political options. If there is a monopolization of political life, with no new ideas and solutions offered to the voters, a low turnout will be a proof of that. Therefore, it is important to maintain the relationship of supervision and accountability between the voters and the elected elite.[247] The electoral system cannot be limited to the "winner takes all", thus not leaving much space to the opposition[248] or the citizens. An election cannot be considered a goal in and on itself, but a means to empower people through their expended representation.[249] Last, but not least, the meaningful representation standard should articulate already existing obligations for the political representation of disadvantaged groups.[250]

Since the general ideas expressed through the meaningful representation standard are omnipresent, the practical arrangements to observe such a standard vary from state to state depending on their realities. Some states have put in place compulsory voting, other states have legislative or party arrangements for a representation of women and minorities, or use referendums and public debates for a verification of their policies, or give a possibility to recall elected representatives.

The more recent changes requiring a balance between the political elites and the voters, between the sexes, between the majority and the minority need a legal reflection at the European level. Articulating a standard of a meaningful representation in the "free and fair" paradigm will mirror those changes in the legal sphere.

If there is a lack of standards by which all the subjects of international law are measured, the only guarantee against arbitrary decisions, driven by the state interests of the decision-making states are to be found in the world three of Karl Popper[251,] i.e., in the world of the ideas. The formula for measuring internal democracy of an international or regional organization cannot only be a simple sum of the number of its member states considered democratic, as suggested

---

[247] Lijphart, Patterns of Democracy (Serbian translation, published by Sluzbeni List CG Beograd)) (1999) pp. 269-275.
[248] Kelly, Monitoring Democracy (2013) p. 142
[249] Beetham, Defining and Measuring Democracy (1994) pp. 70, 116, 127.
[250] Article 7 of CEDAW, Article 5 (c) of CERD, Protocol 12 of ECHR. For minorities see also OSCE/CoE, National Minority Standards (2007).
[251] Unended Quest: An Intellectual Autobiography (Macedonian translation, published by Magor) (1999).

by Pevehose[252]. In the world nowadays, it cannot be expected that democratic states or organizations intuitively always act in accordance with the morality and justice at the international level, even when the respective action is not complementary to the defined national interests. Therefore, some constraints must exist at the international level, which in case of elections should be articulated in a form of specific common election standards.

Ensuring Synergy in the European electoral assistance

The cooperation and coordination among various election support bodies are mentioned, as they represent a key to the effective electoral assistance. They allow for a better use of the resources and provide a bigger leverage in the dialogue with the government(s). Indeed, the examined bodies use various forms to enhance their cooperation mostly at the highest level. However, a strengthened cooperation at the technical and field level will also contribute towards more effective individualized election support according to the country's needs.

A specialized international body mandated with ensuring a meaningful follow-up for remedying the detected electoral weaknesses will represent a solution to the problem. However, the weaknesses noted before and unnecessary expenditure must be avoided, in order to avoid creating just another labyrinth of international bureaucracy.[253]

Such a body should be established in the form of a coordinative secretariat, under the principles of impartiality, professionalism and equitable representation. The above-mentioned trilateral agreement may also include a chapter on the establishment and duties of the coordinative secretariat. This body should be clearly mandated to ensure the follow-up to the election actions instigated by OSCE, CoE and EU regarding a particular country. So, its efforts should not only be focused on making the assessments and recommendations, but on effective manners and procedures to change the states' behaviour in the elections' arena.

In order to fulfil its mandate related to effective electoral reform, the coordinative secretariat should be equipped with the following powers: 1) Fact-finding powers, meaning that it will have access to any type of information either oral or in writing that it deems necessary for whichever country; 2) The ability to receive information and grievances from political parties

---

[252] With a Little Help from my Friends? Regional Organizations and the Consolidation of Democracy, American Political Science Review vol. 46 no. 3 (2002).

[253] For international organizations as bureaucracies that can be controlled to varying degrees by their political masters, see Hawkins, Lake, Nielson, Tierney, Delegations and Agency in International Organizations, Cambridge University Press (2006).

V. Neverending debate: conclusions and recommendations

and NGOs; and 3) The power to issue warnings to the state concerned and public warnings, as well as to propose to the CoE and OSCE political bodies to sanction the state concerned, in accordance with their own rules. However, such a proposal should come only when the state ignores the repeated warnings in relation to serious electoral defects.

These powers are important for a prompt, systematic and flexible response to the election irregularities, in order they to be remedied in the on-going elections. Further, the proposed body could be used as an advisory body for the states when they wish to conduct an electoral reform, as well as for the international organizations when they do their planning for election support.

The coordinative secretariat should keep a single public repository, containing information from the relevant election support bodies, accessible to all organizations and states. The repository will contribute to the improved post electoral coordination and cooperation. In particular, such a database will have all the reports, assessments, recommendations, projects, judgments/decisions, opinions and the reform attempts pertaining to a particular country in a given period of time. It will enable an exchange of information and can be used as an effective tool for planning of projects, resources and expertise, and for ensuring a consistent interpretation and application of the election standards. In addition, the inclusion of the demand side in both the decision-making and the offered expertise will have beneficial effects on the electoral assistance. In consequence, the efforts should no longer be focused only on making the assessments and recommendations, but also on effective manners and procedures to change the states' behavior in the elections' arena. The follow up to recommendations will be done in a structural and consistent manner instead on an *ad hoc* basis.

In order to avoid any duplication of resources and efforts, the secretariat may be placed either within the OSCE/ODIHR, or within the CoE in view of their geographical mandates. In the interviews carried out with the CoE and the OSCE election officials, they agreed that their organizations had to have wider competencies with respect to elections for more effective electoral assistance. It is recommended that the proposed coordinative secretariat be placed under the auspices of the OSCE/ODIHR because of the following reasons: 1) If the body is set up under the CoE auspices, it may have to deal with non-CoE member states, therefore it may risk a lack of mandate; 2) It is the OSCE/ODIHR that has the overall responsibility for election observation in Europe. This body has already created a database of the practice, theory and shortcomings in the electoral area of the OSCE participating states. For its part, the CoE sends only small election observation missions under the auspices of the OSCE/ODIHR; 3) The OSCE/ODIHR has an overall mandate to observe and assist the states in all types of elections, unlike CoE where different bodies are each in charge with a specific type of elections; 4) Whereas the OSCE/ODIHR has technical electoral experts who continuously work on election issues, in CoE election observation is done by politicians, and legislative support by experts – members of its bodies, on *ad hoc* basis; 5) The OSCE has greater election-related capacity in comparison to the CoE, as it not only observes elections, but also conducts, organizes and facilitates election process in conflict regions. It also has field missions whose presence and experience represent a valuable contribution to electoral reforms of the countries where they have been placed; and 6) The secretariat will build on already existing experience, knowledge and resources of the OSCE/ODIHR, thus cutting its costs.

The coordinative secretariat should have a steering committee with permanent members from the OSCE/ODIHR, OSCE/PA, CoE VC, ECtHR, CoE/CLRAE, CoE PA and EU/EP. It may also have temporary members such as from the UN election bodies and representatives from the particular states where election reform is on-going as a follow-up to the CoE and the OSCE/ODIHR recommendations, as well as from the donor states. The steering committee will have decision-making power. It will define general policy and give directions for the work of the coordinative secretariat.

The drawback of establishing a coordinative secretariat within the OSCE/ODIHR is in its cost, as it will require more money from the taxpayers. Therefore, the states might not be willing to pay for yet another body mandated to assist them with their electoral reform. However, the states are willing to pay for electoral observation, for monitoring of their electoral campaign financing and still continue to violate the European election standards. From that view point, it looks like the overall costs of establishing such a body will be lesser than the cost of persisting violations of election standards, which frustrates the purpose of election observation and providing recommendations for electoral reform.

Implications of the Comparative Study

V. Neverending debate: conclusions and recommendations

This analysis departs from the premise that the countries (as electoral units) are the main actors, which safeguard the paradigm of "free and fair elections" in Europe. If any of the countries from the sample were to assess its electoral theory and practice for a compliance with the European election standards, it would have faced the same dilemma:
-*Which tools to use for such an exercise?*

The states have at their disposal election standards developed by the OSCE, the CoE, or even the EU, as measuring tools of electoral quality. However, the state will first have to decide which organization to consider more credible in order to avoid a triple electoral assessment. If it decides that it is a waste of time to assess and re-assess its electoral theory and practice by different sets of tools coming from various European organizations, it may well decide to use European election standards developed under one of the European organizations.

If the state decides to utilize the CoE electoral tools, considering them more credible because of their legal value, it will have to decide which set of the CoE electoral keys opens the magical paradigm of "free and fair elections". As demonstrated above, the CoE election standards encompass a number of different election standards that vary in terms of legal value, specific topic and acceptance by the states. However, when they are examined separately, the results show various lacunae in all sets of the election standards valid for Europe.

The OSCE compilation of election standards from its various documents also contains gaps vis-a-vis the "free and fair elections" paradigm. For instance, the OSCE core election standards do not encompass the independence and impartiality of the EMBs. Thus, vital elements of the electoral measurement may be lacking, if the state is not willing to accept the dispersed OSCE interpretative standards from the secondary sources.

If the state is an EU member, it may select to follow only the EU election standards, which are narrow in the sense that they regulate only a certain type of election, or of an electoral segment.

To sum-up, even if the state has the best intention to abide by the European standards in the electoral field, it will encounter many difficulties in developing legislation and practice consistent with the European election standards.

V. Neverending debate: conclusions and recommendations

The results of the comparative study in light of the hypothesis show that the conceptualized single set of the European standards helps avoid confusion, contradictory interpretations and lacunae, which exist in the current European standards in the election field. Such a common denominator of "free and fair elections" will enable the states to avoid a selective and partial approach towards their electoral legislation and practice. However, it should be acknowledged that a future "standardization process" entails a risk of interference with already well-established election standards. It is this risk precisely, which mitigates against adoption of a comprehensive legally-binding treaty, with an explicit enforcement value. If a trilateral agreement is foreseen as a form for the common denominator of "free and fair elections", the above-mentioned risk might be mitigated by way of discussions with the states, their greater inclusion in the process and preliminary agreements among the CoE, EU and OSCE. Any potential "unwanted" effects of the agreement or objections by the states may be discussed, addressed and resolved at this stage. Solutions to the risks and potential unwanted effects uttered by the states may become part of the agreement itself. For example, the proposed agreement may stipulate that it will not produce direct effect in the EU, albeit a part of the EU law. Empirical evidence show that cooperation agreements regulating modalities of joint actions in the area of democratization and protection of human rights and rule of law have already been concluded in the past by the relevant international organizations. Regarding the election arena, it is worth mentioning the recommendation to sign an agreement on election observation between CoE and OSCE.[254] Furthermore, judging by the mandates of the three international organizations, their member/participating states have expressed a clear intent for them to be involved in safeguarding free and fair elections in Europe. It is clear that on the substantive side, the agreement will undoubtedly further the above objective.

As to the proposed standard of a meaningful representation in political decision-making, the examination shows that it has its roots deeply planted in democratic theories. In addition, some of its segments are already clearly defined in the electoral legislation of France, Slovenia, Belgium and the UK. Its inclusion in the European standards will equal an inclusion of an agent of positive change, affecting not only the mechanics of the electoral process, but going deeply in the spirit of democratic commitment and its sustainability.

---

[254] The CoE and the OSCE: Enhancing co-operation and complementarity through greater coherence, Ulfstein, DPP (2012)1, p. 18 at <http://www. coe.int>.

V. Neverending debate: conclusions and recommendations

The trilateral agreement mentioned above should contain all the elements of "free and fair elections" conceptualized and proposed in the Dissertation, minus the meaningful representation standard, if it to be of any value for the states. There are multiple reasons in favour of such a proposal. All elements that make the European election standards are in one way or another already valid for the European continent. They have already been agreed upon by the states. Therefore, it makes no sense to start re-negotiating the same electoral standards. The main aim for the conceptualization of European standards in the election field is not just to produce a simple inventory, but to craft a tool that can be effectively used by the states while undertaking electoral reform and implementing election standards. Clearly spelling out the conceptualized standards for "free and fair elections" in a single document, signed by all organizations that have developed them (with their members' consent), will help avoid future disputes about the meaning and interpretation of those standards. In addition, these standards are valid, have been already used and continue to be used in election observation and in the election legislation reforms.

In view of the fact that certain elections take place right after a conflict or in a tense security situation, the agreement may foresee an exception to some election standards for security and safety reasons. Such an exception, as invoked by a state, should be examined on case-by-case basis by a European body that should have the power to decide whether or not such an exception is legitimate or not before elections take place. As an example, the conceptualized election standards foresee a repetition of elections, whenever they have been annulled. However, an exception to this rule is legitimate when repeated voting poses a threat to the security of the people, provided that the outcome of those elections would not have any impact on the overall results. Similarly, the counting might be better done in a counting centre with the results publicized there, if counting in the polling stations represents too high a security risk. The counting should be done only in presence of accredited observers, if transparency poses security risks for the operation. Furthermore, whereas the five years election interval might be prolonged in case of public emergency, the period of prolongation should be legitimized with the coordinative secretariat.

Any security and safety exceptions must be compiled and made public. The coordinative secretariat is the best-placed body to deal with the cases where extenuating circumstances that may lower election standards exist. Primarily, because no other body has such *ex-ante* power. Secondarily, the proposed secretariat is conceived as a cross-organizational body, mandated with the observance of common European standards. On one hand, the above-proposed solution will provide sufficient flexibility to address any state-specific security and political concerns. On the other hand, it will act as a watchdog against lowering the European "free and fair elections" standard.

The results from the research show that all states from the sample have been invited at the inter-governmental level to remedy different aspect of their elections. Despite the fact that some of the states have received considerable attention by the international bodies mandated to propagate "free and fair elections", the pace of the implementation of the recommendations has been very slow. On one hand, it does not appear that the lack of resources and funds was ever invoked as an excuse. On the other hand, historico-geographic factors and cultural divergence have been used as an excuse for not bringing the legislation up to compliance with the regional election standards.

In a reply to the states' sovereignty argument, it is reiterated that the election standard of "free and fair elections" in Europe conceptualized above contains what has already been agreed upon by the states at the European level. Even for the newly proposed standard of a meaningful representation, the bases have been laid down, previously. Therefore, the states should take legislative, judicial, administrative and other measures to translate the conceptualized election standards into electoral practice for all types of elections. The primary focus of the conceptualized election standards is on how to enable a free expression of the will of people -which represents the basis of sovereignty. The conceptualized election standards thus leave room to the states to elect their electoral system, electoral threshold, forms and procedures for various legal remedies, the types of financial and media supervision, conditions for exercising election rights, minorities' representation, sentencing policy as long as they fall within the scope of the standards agreed upon at the European level. The conceptualized election standards do not propose a single electoral model or a single electoral solution ready-made for all. That would be impossible in view of the diversity of conditions in which elections take place in Europe. However, elections that are enabling free expression of the will of people as the basis of sovereignty can take place only when certain principles and conditions are present. Those principles and conditions have been spelt out in the conceptualized election standards proposed herein.

V. Neverending debate: conclusions and recommendations

As to the second limb of the Hypothesis, a European body specialized in electoral reform might prove a useful tool with respect to all countries from the sample, because of the following reasons:

The coordinative secretariat mentioned-above will ensure greater leverage for the regional organizations to inspire the states to implement the recommendations given by various European bodies. Furthermore, it may provide an electoral reform roadmap for the states by assembling the puzzle of recommendations and judgments issued in their case. It will also provide a consistent interpretation of the election standards. Thereby, a partial and slow process of electoral reform will be replaced by a holistic and intensive process. Such an approach will ban the states from (ab)using electoral reform and amending some parts of the legislation contrary to the European election standards, while implementing few recommendations. Still, the electoral assistance must always be provided in balance with the states' sovereignty. Therefore, a key to a success of the proposed specialized election follow-up body would be its impartiality, dedication and commitment of its members to "free and fair elections" in compliance with the international electoral standards.

To conclude, European election standards set out in a trilateral agreement will define the threshold for the states of what should be accepted as "free and fair elections". Effective assistance for electoral reform based on an individualized approach for each of the states requires the use of a holistic method by future specialized coordinative secretariat under the auspices of the OSCE/ODIHR. Finally, acceptance of the election standards for each part of the cycle as part of the political and legal culture of the states should be the end result of such an exercise

Annexes

Disaggregated data per country

CF = campaign financing irregularities

CFR = campaign financing reporting problem

CNR = candidates' nomination restrictions

CTI = non transparent and problematic counting and tallying of results

EC = restricted electoral campaign

I = impunity

II = improper implementation of law

IC = intimidation of candidates

IV = intimidation of voters

LD = legislative deficiency

LR = inadequate and ineffective legal remedies

MA = unequal access to media

MAR = misuse of administrative resources

MB = media biased reporting

PDEMBs = partial and dependent EMBs

PI = police intimidation

PM = inadequate inclusion of minorities

PR = lack of publishing of results

PSA = access to PS

PP = lack of public or accurate protocols

PW = low participation of women

RO = restrictions on election observation

RVR = restricted voting rights

VI = vote inequality

VER = violation of election rights (family, proxy, multiple and group voting, ballot boxes staffing, ballots tampering, vote buying)

VL = voters' list incomplete/ inaccurate

VPI = voting procedures irregularities

UV = breach of universality of vote

Participating state[255]	Year	Problems detected
Albania	1996	II; VL; RO; PI, MA; MB; PDEMBs; VPI; VER; PP; CTI
	1997	VL: CTI; IC; IV
	2000	LD; MA; LR; VPI; VL
	2001	VER; PDEMBs; MB; PI; PW; IC; IV
	2003 and 2004	LD; VL;VER; I; PSA; MA; PW
	2005	IV; IC; MAR; VER; II; I; PDEMBS; RO; VL; MB; LR; PW; PM
	2007	IC; IV; II; CFR; PDEMBs; VL; I; MB; LR; PW; PM; RO; CTI
	2009	IC; IV; CFR; CTI; II; PDEMBs; I; RO; VL, MB; LR; PW; PM
	2011	IC; IV; CFR; CTI; II; PDEMBs; I; VL; MB; LR; PM; VER; CNR
	2013	Report not yet published
Andorra	2011-NAM[256]	CFR, VI; RO
Armenia	1996	PI; IV; CTI; PDEMBs; MB
	1998	LD; VI; CI; PDEMBs; RO; MB
	1999	LD; I; IV; IC; LR; PDEMBs; VL; CTI
	2003 (2 reports)	VER; I; MB; IV; PR; RO; LD; LR; VL; PSA
	2007	LD; I; LR; PDEMBs; MB; VI; PW; VER; MB; VL; PR; MAR; ECR; EC; CF

---

[255] ODIHR election observation and assessment. The participating states have been selected on the basis of their CoE membership. The focus is on the type of irregularities, and no distinction is made between the types of election.

[256] Needs assessment mission.

	2008	IV; VER; RVR; VL; PDEMBs; MAR; MA; MB LR; CFR; PSA; VPI
	2012	VER; I; II; VL; LER; PW; PSA; UV; CFR; EC
	2013	I; UV; VL; LD; CF; MB; LR; RO; PSA; VER; MAR
Austria	2009-expert report	LD
	2010	VPI; LD; RO; LR
	2013	Report not yet published
Azerbaijan	1995	EC; VER; MB; RO; VPI; CTI; CNR
	1998	LD; PDEMBs; II; VL; MAR; RO; MB; VER; EC
	2000 and 2001	PDEMBs; LD; I; PR; LR; VL; MAR; MB; RO; VPI; VER
	2003	VER; I; IC; PI; PDEMBs; LR; PW; BM; EC
	2005	PDEMBs; LR; IC; VL; CTI; PW; VER
	2006	IV; RO; PDEMBs; LR; MB; VPI; VER; CTI; PSA; MA
	2008	LD, PDEMBs; VL; CNR; EC; MB; LR; VER; MA
	2010	CNR; PDEMBs; MB; CTI; VER; LR; PW; VI
Belarus	2001	LD; LR; PDEMBs; IC; MA; VL; VPI; RO
	2004	CF; CTI; LD; II; CNR; IV; PDEMBs; MB; MA
	2006	LD; I; IV; IC; PDEMBs; VPI; VL; EC; CF
	2008	EC; LD; PDEMBs; CNR; MB; LR; VPI
	2010	PDEMBs; EC; IC; LD; MB; VL; CF; RO LR; CTI
	2012	PDEMBs; LR; CNI; CTI; VL; IC; LD; II; RO
Belgium	2007	VPI (E-vote)
	2006	VPI (E-vote)
Bosnia and Herzegovina	1996	CTI; LR; IC; IV
	1997 (2 reports)	VL; PR; VER; MA; MB; LR; LD; VPI; CNR; CFR
	1998	VL; LD; PR; VPR
	2002	LD; MP; LR; VL
	2004	I; LD; PR
	2006	CNI; EC; CTI; PW
	2008-NAM	No particular concerns
	2010	I, MB; PW; VER; CFR
Bulgaria	1997	LD; VL; CNR; CF
	2001	PM; VER; VPI; CF
	2005	LD; EC; VER; VPI
	2006	LD; PDEMBs; VL; VER; CTI; EC
	2009	VER; LD; I; MA; LR; PM
	2011	I; LD; EC; PDEMBs; VL; IV; LR; CTI; PM
	2013	VL; VER; PM; LR; UV
Croatia	1997 (2 reports)	LD; VER; II; VI; RO; VL; MA; IC; IV; EC; PDEMBs; MB; PI; MAR
	2000	UV; VPI; PM; VL; LD; MB; LR; VER; PSA
	2001	LD; LR; PM; PDEMBs; MB; VER; CFR; CNI
	2003	LD; I; MP; VPI; CTI; MB
	2007	LD; II; CFR; MB
	2009-2010	VL; EC; LD; I; CFR; LR
	2011	LD; VL
Cyprus	2001 - expert report	No particular concerns
	2011	PW; LD; CF
	2013	PW; CF; LD
Czech Rep.	1998	LD
	2002	RO; LD; VL; II; LR; MA
	2009 –(2 reports)	LD, CNR
	2010-NAM	CF
	2013	CNR; VL; CFR; LR; I; RO; VPI

Denmark	2009	LD; CFR
	2011-NAM	LD; LR; MA
Estonia	1999	CNR
	2003-NAM	MP
	2007	EC; MP; VPI (e-vote)
	2009	CNR
	2011	MP; MAR; EC; CFR; PL; PW
Finland	2007-NAM	CFR
	2011	CNR; LR; VI; MA
	2012-NAM	CNR; LR
France	2002	MP; RO
	2007	LD; VPI; VL
	2012 (2 reports – NAM)	LR; VPI; LD
Georgia	1999	LD; VI; VL; PDEMBs; II; CF; CNR; IV; IC; VPI; PR; LR
	2000	MAR; LD; PDEMBs; VL; CNR; MA; MB; PI; VER; CTI
	2003	VER; VL; MAR; MA; MB; PDEMBs; VPI; CTI
	2004 (2 reports)	VER; VL; MAR; MA; MB; PDEMBs; VPI; CTI; LR; IO
	2006	MAR; LD; LR; VL; VPI; CTI
	2008 (2 reports)	IC; MAR; CTI; PDEMBs; VL; LD; PW; MB; MA; VER; VPI; LR
	2010	LD; VI; CNR; RVR; VL; IC; MAR; MA; MB; LD; VER; CTI; PW
	2012	EC; IV; IC; LD; VI; LR; VL; II; RO
	2013 (interim report)	No assessment
Germany	2009 (2 reports)	LR; LD; CFR; RO
Greece	2009 (2 reports)	PW; VER; VPI; RO, CNR
	2012	RO; CNR; VL; PW; IMA; CF; CFR
Hungary	1998	LD
	2002	PDEMBs; II; CNR; MB; MA; CFR; LR; PM
	2010	VI; VER; PM; CNR; CFR; CF
Iceland	2009	LD; VI
	2013-NAM	RO; VI; LD
Ireland	2007	CF; EC; VL;RO
	2009-EP	No particular concerns
	2011-NAM	CFR; PM; LR; PW
Italy	2006	MAR; LR; MA; MB; LD
	2008	LD; LR; MA; MB; PW
	2013-NAM	PW; CNR; MB; MA; LR; LD; CFR
	2007	CNR; RVR; UV; MA; LD; PR; PDEMBs; MAR; IC; LR; RO; PW; PM; I; VL; LR; CF; IV
	2009	CF; CI; MAR; UV; MB; MA; VER; VL; II; CTI; PR
	2010	LD; CNR; UV; VL; RVR; IC; MA; MB; LR; CTI; PP
Latvia	1998	LD; PI; VPI; VI; VER; CTI; PR
	2002	PI; CF; VER
	2006	PM; CFR; VER; CNR
	2009-EP	No particular concerns
	2010	CNR; MAR; MB; MA; PW; CTI; UV
	2011	CNR; VI; RVR; PM
Lichtenstein	2009-NAM	LD; PW
Lithuania	1996	VPI; VER; PM
	2009-NAM	No particular concerns

	2012	RO; IV; PM; CFR
Luxemburg	2009-EP	No particular concerns
	2013-NAMP	No particular concerns
Macedonia	1998	LD; MB; VPI; VER; VL; CF
	1999	LD; MB; VPI; VER
	2000	IC; IV; VER; LD; II; MB
	2002	IC; IV; II; MB; MA; LD
	2004	VER; LD; VL; PM; CTI; LR; I
	2005	VER; UI; UV; II; IC; IV; MB; PW
	2006	IV; VER; II; CFR; CF; IC; MAR; PM; MB; MA; LR; CTI
	2008	II; IV; CFR; MB; MA; LR; MAR; I; IC
	2009	IV; PDEMBs; VER; PM; WP; LR; CTI
	2011	LD; VPI; VL; PM; MB; CF; MAR; VI; LR
	2013	DPEMBs; MAR; VI; VL; LR; MB
Malta	2009 - EP	LR
	2013	RO; CNR; CFR; LR; LD; MB
Moldova	1996	LD; VL; VPI
	1998	UV; LD; VL; MA; MB
	2001	VER; PR; CTI; MA; VL; PM; EC
	2003	MB; IC; MAR; CF
	2005	MA; RVR; IV; PI; CF; LD; PM; CTI; DPEMBs
	2007	MA; CNR; RVR; CF; CFR; MB; LD; PW; I; II; VL
	2009 (2 reports)	IC; IV; MB; CF; MAR; PR; LD; VL; PR; CRI; LR
	2010	LD; II; I; VPI; VL; PW
	2011	VL; CF; LD; CFR; CTI; VER; LR
Monaco	2013	UV; CNR; CFR; RO
Montenegro	1997	LD; IV; II
	1998	LR; VL; MA
	2000	MB; LD; PDEMBs; LR; VL; CNR
	2001	PI; PM; II; IV; LD
	2002 (2 reports)	CNR; MAR; LD; IDEMBs; PM; PW; CF; EC
	2003 (2 reports)	LD; MAR; IV; VER; MA
	2006	LD; CF; VER; PW
	2008	MAR; I
	2009	MAR; I; PM; LD; UV; VL
	2012	VL; CFR; LR; MAR; II; MB
	2013	MAR; LD; UV; CFR; CF; VL; MA; MB
Netherlands	2006	CFR; VPI (e-vote)
	2009	CNR
	2010	LR; CFR
	2012	LD; CFR; LR
Norway	2009	VL; CNR; LR; VER; PM
	2011	Internet voting technical comments
Poland	2007	MA; MB; VP; VER
	2009 – EP	LD
	2011	VP; CNR; CFR; EC; LR; VER
Portugal	2009	CNR; VI; VL; RO
Romania	1996	II; LD; VL
	2000	PM; PW; LD; RO; CFR
	2004	LR; PR; VPI; MAR; CF; MA; LD; RO; PR; PM
	2009 (2 reports – EP)	VPI; PR
	2012	RO; CF; PM
Russia	1996	CF; MB; MAR
	1999	IC; PR; MB; MAR; II

	2000	CF; MB; MA; MAR; VPI; II
	2003	MAR; CF; VER; I; CNR; MA; II
	2004	VER; CF; MB; MAR; VI; CNR; CTI
	2011	CNR; MB; IV; VER; PR; II; LD; DPEMBs; MA; MAR; IC; RO; CTI; IU; LR
	2012	MB; CTI; DPEMBs; CTI; VL; LR
San Marino	2012	CF; LR; VPI; PW; RO; CNR
Serbia	1997	LD; II; PDEMBs
	2000	MB
	2002 (2 reports)	VER; MP; RO; DL; CF
	2003	VL; VR; VPI; LD; CNR; UV
	2004	II; MW; MA
	2007	PDEMBs; LD; II
	2008 (2 reports)	LD; II; CF; CFR; RO; LR; VL
	2012	CFR; MB; VL; VER; PDEMBs; LR; RO; VI; PM; VER; I
Slovak Rep.	1998	MB; LD; PDEMBs; CNR; RO
	1999	LD
	2002	LD; I; II; LR; CF; RO; PR; RSR; MA; PM
	2004	LD; LR; MA; CFR; I; PM
	2010	LD; II; CF; CFR; PM; PW; LR; VER
	2012 – NAM	CFR; PM
Slovenia	2009 – EP	CNR, LD
	2011	RO; EAM; VI; CFR; MA; PSA
Spain	2004	VER; RO
	2008	VPI; VI; MA
	2009 – EP	CNR
	2011	VI; CNR; CFR; MA
Sweden	2009 – EP	CNR, LD; CFR
	2010-NAM	RO; CFR; PM
Switzerland	2007	CFR; RO
	2011	LD
Turkey	2002	PM; LD; RO
	2007	LD; LR; MP
	2011	VI; CF; IC; PW; CNR
Ukraine	1998	MAR; CI; VI; PM; LD; MB; MA; VER; VPI; LR
	1999	LR; MB; MAR; MA; VPI; VER; CTI
	2002	VER; MA; MB; LR; IV; IC; MAR; PDEMBs; CF; LD; PR; VL
	2004	MAR; CF; VER; PI; IV; UV; ER
	2006	LR; VPI; LD; CFR; VL
	2007	VL; LD; RVR; VPI; LR; IV; PDEMBs; MA
	2010	VER; MAR; CTI; II; I; MB; LR
	2012	MAR; CFR; MB; MA; CTI; I; MB; VER; LD; CF; PP; VL; CNR; IC; LR; RO; DPEMBs; PW; IV
UK	2003	RO; VPI; EC; VL
	2005	LD; RO; VPI
	2010	LD; RO; VPI

FREQUENCY OF IRREGULARITIES

Low = L (40 <); Middle = M (40-80); High = H (< 80)

High frequency
-LD; -LR; -MB

Middle frequency
-VER; -VL; -CTI; -RO;
-CFR; -MAR; -VPI; -MA;
PDEMBs;   -CF;   -CNR

Low frequency
-RVR; -EC; -I; -PW; -IV
-PR; -VI;   -II; -IC   -PI   -PM

Relevant articles of the UN Human Rights instruments

Name of the UN instrument	Entry into force	Text of relevant articles
Charter of the United Nation	24.10.1945	**Article 73** Members of the United Nations which have or assume responsibilities for the administration of territories whose peoples have not yet attained a full measure of self-government recognize the principle that the interests of the inhabitants of these territories are paramount, and accept as a sacred trust the obligation to promote to the utmost, within the system of international peace and security established by the present Charter, the well-being of the inhabitants of these territories, and, to this end: ... b. to develop self-government, to take due account of the political aspirations of the peoples, and to assist them in the progressive development of their free political institutions, according to the particular circumstances of each territory and its peoples and their varying stages of advancement... **Article 76** The basic objectives of the trusteeship system, in accordance with the Purposes of the United Nations laid down in Article 1 of the present Charter, shall be: ... b. to promote the political, economic, social, and educational advancement of the inhabitants of the trust territories, and their progressive development towards self-government or independence as may be appropriate to the particular circumstances of each territory and its peoples and the freely addressed wishes of the peoples concerned, and as may be provided by in the terms of each trusteeship agreement...
The Universal Declaration of Human Rights	adopted on 10.12.1948	**Article 21** (1) Everyone has the right to take part in the government of his country, directly or through freely chosen representatives. (2) Everyone has the right of equal access to public service to his country. (3) The will of the people shall be the basis of the authority of government; this will shall be expressed in periodic and genuine elections which shall be by universal and equal suffrage and shall

		be held by secret vote or by equivalent free voting procedure.
International Covenant on Civil and Political Rights	23.3.1976	**Article 25** Every citizen shall have the right and the opportunity, without any of the distinctions mentioned in article 2 and without unreasonable restrictions: (a) To take part in the conduct of public affairs, directly or through freely chosen representatives; (b) To vote and to be elected at genuine periodic elections which shall be by universal and equal suffrage and shall be held by secret ballot, guaranteeing the free expression of the will of the electors; (c) To have access, on general terms of equality, to public service in his country.
Convention for Elimination of all Forms of Discrimination against Women	3.9.1981	**Article 7** States Parties shall take all appropriate measures to eliminate discrimination against women in the political and public life of the country and, in particular, shall ensure to women, on equal terms with men, the right: (a) To vote in all elections and public referenda and to be eligible for election to all publicly elected bodies; (b) To participate in the formulation of government policy and the implementation thereof and to hold public office and perform all public functions at all levels of government; (c) To participate in non-governmental organizations and associations concerned with the public and political life of the country. **Article 8** States Parties shall take all appropriate measures to ensure to women, on equal terms with men and without any discrimination, the opportunity to represent their Governments at the international level and to participate in the work of international organizations.
Convention for Elimination of all Forms of Racial Discrimination	4.1.1969	**Article 5** In compliance with the fundamental obligations laid down in article 2 of this Convention, States Parties undertake to prohibit and to eliminate racial discrimination in all its forms and to guarantee the right of everyone, without distinction as to race, color, or national or ethnic origin, to equality before the law, notably in the enjoyment of the following rights: ... (c) Political rights, in particular the right to participate in elections-to vote and to stand for election-on the basis of universal and equal suffrage, to take part in the Government as well as in the conduct of public affairs at any level and to have equal access to public service...
Convention on the Rights of Persons with Disabilities	3.5.2008	**Article 29** States Parties shall guarantee to persons with disabilities political rights and the opportunity to enjoy them on an equal basis with others, and shall undertake to: (a) Ensure that persons with disabilities can effectively and fully participate in political and public life on an equal basis with others, directly or through freely chosen representatives, including the right and opportunity for persons with disabilities to vote and be elected, inter alia, by: (i) Ensuring that voting procedures, facilities and materials are appropriate, accessible and easy to understand and use; (ii) Protecting the right of persons with disabilities to vote by secret ballot

Annexes

		in elections and public referendums without intimidation, and to stand for elections, to effectively hold office and perform all public functions at all levels of government, facilitating the use of assistive and new technologies where appropriate; (iii) Guaranteeing the free expression of the will of persons with disabilities as electors and to this end, where necessary, at their request, allowing assistance in voting by a person of their own choice; (b) Promote actively an environment in which persons with disabilities can effectively and fully participate without discrimination and on an equal basis with others, and encourage their participation in public affairs, including: (i) Participation in non-governmental organizations and associations concerned with the public and political life of the country, and in the activities and administration of political parties; (ii) Forming and joining organizations of persons with disabilities to represent persons with disabilities at international, national, regional and local levels.
Convention on the Protection of the Rights of All Migrant Workers and Members of Their Families	1.7.2003	Article 41 1. Migrant workers and members of their families shall have the right to participate in public affairs of their State of origin and to vote and to be elected at elections of that State, in accordance with its legislation. 2. The States concerned shall, as appropriate and in accordance with their legislation, facilitate the exercise of these rights. Article 42 1. States Parties shall consider the establishment of procedures or institutions through which account may be taken, both in States of origin and in States of employment, of special needs, aspirations and obligations of migrant workers and members of their families and shall envisage, as appropriate, the possibility for migrant workers and members of their families to have their freely chosen representatives in those institutions. 2. States of employment shall facilitate, in accordance with their national legislation, the consultation or participation of migrant workers and members of their families in decisions concerning the life and administration of local communities. 3. Migrant workers may enjoy political rights in the State of employment if that State, in the exercise of its sovereignty, grants them such rights.

Judgments of ECtHR relevant for elections

Ordinal no.	Judgments
1	*Matthews v. UK, Application no. 24833/94, judgment of 18 February 1999
2	*Labita v. Italy, Application no. 26772/95, judgment of 6 April 2000
3	*Gaulieder v. Slovakia, Application no. 36909/97, judgment of 18 May 2000
4	*Rafah Partisi and Others v. Turkey, Application nos. 41340/98-41344/98, judgment of 31 July 2001
5	*Podkolzina v. Latvia, Application no. 46726/00, judgment of 9 April 2002
6	*Selim Sadak and Others v. Turkey, Application nos. 25144/94; 26149/95-26154/95, 27100/95 and 27101/95, judgment of 11 June 2002
7	*Refah Partisi and Others v. Turkey, Application nos. 41340/98, 41342/98, 41343/98 and 41344/98, judgment of 13 February 2003
8	*De Savoie v. Italy, Application no. 53360/99, judgment of 24 April 2003
9	*Hirst v. UK, Application no. 74025/01, judgment of 30 March 2004
10	*Zdanoka v. Latvia, Application no. 58278/00, judgment of 17 June 2004
11	*Aziz v. Cyprus, Application no. 69949/01, judgment of 22 June 2004
12	*Santoro v. Italy, Application no. 36681/97, judgment of 1 July 2004
13	*Melnychenko v. Ukraine, Application no. 17707/02, judgment of 19 October 2004
14	*Gorzelik and Others v. Poland, Application no. 44158/98, judgment of …2004
15	*PY v. France, Application no. 66289/01, judgment of 11 January 2005
16	*Hirst v. UK (No. 2), Application no. 74025/01, judgment of 6 October 2005
17	*Zdanoka v. Latvia, Application no. 58278/00, judgment of 16 March 2006
18	*Albanese v. Italy, Application no. 77924/01, judgment of 23 March 2006
19	*Campagnano v. Italy, Application no. 77955/01, judgment of 23 March 2006
20	*Vitiello v. Italy, Application no. 77962/01, judgment of 23 March 2006
21	*Sykhovetskyy v. Ukraine, Application no. 13716/02, judgment of 28 March 2006
22	*Fazilet Partisi and Kutan v. Turkey Application no. 1444/02, judgment of 27 April 2006
23	*Bova v. Italy, Application no. 25513/02, judgment of 24 May 2006
24	*Pantuso v. Italy, Application no. 21120/02, judgment of 24 May 2006
25	*Collarile v Italy, Application no. 10644/02, judgment of 8 June 2006
26	*Lykourezos v. Greece, Application no. 33554/03, judgment of 15 June 2006
27	*Chiumiento v. Italy, Application no. 3649/02, judgment of 29 June 2006
28	*La Frazia v. Italy, Application no. 3653/02, judgment of 29 June 2006
29	*Vertucci v. Italy, Application no. 2987/02, judgment of 29 June 2006
30	*Campello v. Italy, Application no. 21757/02, judgment of 6 July 2006
31	*Vincenzo Taiani v. Italy, Application no. 36380/02, judgment of 13 July 2006
32	*Taiani v. Italy, Application no. 3641/02, judgment of 20 July 2006
33	*Gasser v. Italy, Application no. 10481/02, judgment of 21 September 2006
34	*De Blasi v. Italy, Application no. 1595/02, judgment of 5 October 2006
35	*Linkov v. Czech Republic, Application no. 10504/03, judgment of 7 December 2006
36	*Russian Conservative Party of Entrepreneurs and others v. Russia, Application no. 55066/00, judgment of 11 January 2007
37	*Yumak and Sadak v. Turkey, Application no. 10226/03, judgment of 30 January 2007
38	*Kavakci v. Turkey, Application no. 71907/01, judgment of 5 April 2007
39	*Silay v. Turkey, Application no. 8691/02, judgment of 5 April 2007
40	*Ilicak v. Turkey, Application no. 15294/02, judgment of 5 April 2007
41	*Krasnov and Skuratov v. Russia, Application no. 17864/04, 21396/04, judgment of 19 July 2007

42	*Party Nationalist Basque v. France, Application no. 71251/01, judgment of 7 September 2007
43	*Sobaci v. Turkey, Application no. 26733/02, judgment of 29 November 2007
44	*Sarukhanyan v. Armenia, Application no. 39878/03, judgment of 27 May 2008
45	*Calmanovici v. Romania, Application no. 42250/02, judgment of 1 July 2008
46	*Kovach v. Ukraine, Application no. 39424/02, judgment of 7 February 2008
47	*Paschalidis, Koutmeridis and Zaharakis v. Greece, Application nos. 27863/05, 28422/05, 28028/05, judgment of 10 April 2008
48	Adamsons v. Latvia, Application no. 3669/03, judgment of 24 June 2008
49	*The Georgian Labor Party v. Georgia, Application no. 9103/04, judgment of 8 July 2008
50	*Yumak and Sadak v. Turkey, Application no. 10226/03, judgment of 8 July 2008
51	*Tanase and Chirtoaca v. Moldova, Application no. 7/08, judgment of 18 November 2008
52	*Adamsons v. Latvia, Application no. 3669/03, judgment of 1 December 2008
53	*Petkov v. Bulgaria, Application nos. 77568/01, 178/02, 505/02, judgment of 11 June 2009
54	*Herritaren Zerrenda v. Spain, Application no. 43518/04, judgment of 30 June 2009
55	*Etxeberria Barrena Arza Nafarroako Autodeterminazio Bilgunea and Aiarako and Others v. Spain, Application nos. 35579/03, 35613/03, 35626/03 and 35634/03, judgment of 30 June 2009
56	*Herri Batasuna and Batasuna v. Spain, Application nos. 25803/04 and 25817/04, judgment of 30 June 2009.
57	*Seyidzade v. Azerbaijan, Application no. 37700/05, judgment of 3 December 2009
58	*Sejdik and Finci v. B&H, Applications nos. 2766/06 and 34386/06, judgment of 22 December 2009
59	*Grosar v. Romania, Application no. 78039/01, judgment of 2 March 2010
60	*Namat Aliyev v. Azerbaijan, Application no. 18705/06, judgment of 8 April 2010
61	*Frodl v. Austria, Application no. 20201/04, Judgment of 8 April 2010
62	*Alajos Kiss v. Hungary, Application no. 38832/06, judgment of 20 May 2010
63	*Sitaropoulos and Others v. Greece, Application no. 42202/07, judgment of 8 July 2010
64	*Kerimova v. Azerbaijan, Application no. 20799/06, judgment of 30 September 2010
65	*Greens and M.T. v. the United Kingdom, Application no. 60041/08, judgment of 23 November 2010
66	*Paksas v. Lithuania, Application no. 34932/04, judgment of 6 January 2011
67	*Scoppola v. Italy, Application no. 126/05, judgment of 18 January 2011
68	*Orujov v. Azerbaijan, Application no. 4508/06, judgment of 26 July 2011
69	*Hajili v. Azerbaijan, Application no. 6984/06, judgment of 6 December 2011
70	*Kerimli and Alibeyli v. Azerbaijan, Application nos. 18475/06, 22444/06, judgment of 6 December 2011
71	*Mammadov v. Azerbaijan (No. 2) Application no. 4641/06, judgment of 10 April 2012
72	*Khanhuseyn Aliyev v. Azerbaijan, Application no. 19554/06, judgment of 21 May 2012
73	*Atakishi v. Azerbaijan, Application no. 18469/06, judgment of 28 May 2012
74	* Ekoglasnost v. Bulgaria, Application no. 30386/05, judgment of 6 November 2012
75	*Cucu v. Romania, Application no. 22362/06, judgment of 13 November 2012

BIBLIOGRAPHY

Accetto, ACCESS TO ELECTORAL RIGHTS SLOVENIA (2013)

Accetto, UNITED IN CRISIS: THE DEVELOPMENT OF THE EUROPEAN UNION THROUGH CONCRETE PROBLEMS (2009)

Bogdanor, LEGITIMACY, ACCOUNTABILITY AND DEMOCRACY IN THE EUROPEAN UNION, A Federal Trust Report (2007)

Council of Europe, CODE OF GOOD PRACTICE IN ELECTORAL MATTERS, ADOPTED GUIDELINES AND EXPLANATORY REPORT, CoE EUROPEAN COMMISSION FOR DEMOCRACY THROUGH LAW, 9CDL-EL(2002)5

Dahl, A PREFACE TO DEMOCRATIC THEORY (3rd edition) (2006)

Dahl, WHAT POLITICAL INSTITUTIONS DOES LARGE-SCALE DEMOCRACY REQUIRE? Political Science Quarterly vol. 120, no. 2 (2005)

D'Amato, INTERNATIONAL LAW ANTHOLOGY (1994)

Dimitrieva, EVROPSKA POVELJA O LOKALNOJ SAMOUPRAVI, IMPLEMENTACIJA EVROPSKE POVELJE O LOKALNOJ SAMOUPRAVI U REPUBLICI HRVATSKOJ, Simpozij Osijek (1998)

Elklit, Svensson, A FRAMEWORK FOR THE SYSTEMATIC STUDY OF ELECTION QUALITY (2005)

Elklit, Svensson, THE RISE OF ELECTION MONITORING: WHAT MAKES ELECTIONS FREE AND FAIR? (1997)

Franck, FAIRNESS IN THE INTERNATIONAL LEGAL AND INSTITUTIONAL SYSTEM (General Course on Public International Law), Academy of International Law Offprint from the Recueil des course, Vol. 240 (1993 – III)

Franck, THE EMERGING RIGHT TO DEMOCRATIC GOVERNANCE, The American Journal of International Law, Vol 86, No. 1 (1992) pp. 46-91

Gallagher, Laver, Mair, REPRESENTATIVE GOVERNMENT IN MODERN EUROPE (fifth edition) (2011)

Ghebali, DEBATING ELECTION AND ELECTION MONITORING STANDARD AT THE OSCE: BETWEEN TECHNICAL NEEDS AND POLITICIZATION (2006)

Goodwin-Gill, FREE AND FAIR ELECTIONS (2006)

Grad, Svete, Lumbar, PREDPISE O VOLITVAH V DRZAVNI ZBOR 2008 (2008)

Harris, Boyle, Warbrick, LAW OF THE EUROPEAN CONVENTION ON HUMAN RIGHTS (1995)

Harvey, MILITANT DEMOCRACY AND THE EUROPEAN CONVENTION ON HUMAN RIGHTS, European Law Review (2004)

Howard, Roessler, LIBERALIZING ELECTORAL OUTCOMES IN COMPETITIVE AUTHORITARIAN REGIMES, American Political Science Review vol. 50 no. 2 (2006)

Ishay, THE HUMAN RIGHTS READER: MAJOR POLITICAL WRITINGS, ESSAYS, SPEECHES AND DOCUMENTS FROM THE BIBLE TO THE PRESENT (Macedonian translation published by MI-AN) (1997)

Jacobs, White, Ovey, THE EUROPEAN CONVENTION ON HUMAN RIGHTS (4th edition) (2004)

Karakamisheva, INTERNATIONAL AND EUROPEAN ELECTION STANDARDS WITH SPECIAL FOCUS ON THE CODE OF THE VENICE COMMISSION FOR GOOD PRACTICE IN ELECTORAL MATTERS (…)

Kelly, MONITORING DEMOCRACY (2013)

Kochenov, BEHIND THE COPENHAGEN FACADE. THE MEANING AND STRUCTURE OF THE COPENHAGEN POLITICAL CRITERION OF DEMOCRACY AND THE RULE OF LAW, European Integration Online Papers vol. 8 (2004)

Levitsky, Way, AUTOCRACY BY DEMOCRATIC RULES: THE DYNAMICS OF COMPETITIVE AUTHORITARIANISM IN THE POST COLD WAR ERA (rev. 2003)

Lijphart, PATTERNS OF DEMOCRACY (Serbian translation, published by Sluzbeni List CG Beograd) (1999)

Miller, THE BLACKWELL ENCYCLOPEDIA OF POLITICAL THOUGHT (Macedonian translation, published by MI-AN) (2002)

Pevehose, WITH A LITTLE HELP FROM MY FRIENDS? REGIONAL ORGANIZATIONS AND THE CONSOLIDATION OF DEMOCRACY, American Political Science Review vol. 46 no. 3 (2002)

Popper, UNENDED QUEST: AN INTELLECTUAL AUTOBIOGRAPHY (Macedonian, published by Magor) (1999)

Roth, GOVERNMENTAL ILLEGITIMACY IN INTERNATIONAL LAW (2000)

Sancin, BRIEFING PAPER ON RESPONSIBILITY TO PROTECT (2011)

Sancin, Kovacic (ed.) RESPONSIBILITY TO PROTECT IN THEORY IN PRACTICE (2013)

Steiner, Alston, INTERNATIONAL HUMAN RIGHTS IN CONTEXT, LAW, POLITICS, MORALS (2nd edition) (2000)

Van Dijk, Hoof, THEORY AND PRACTICE OF THE EUROPEAN CONVENTION ON HUMAN RIGHTS (1998)

Web sites

ACE ELECTORAL KNOWLEDGE NETWORK: <http://aceproject.org>

BEYONDINTRACTABILITY, official web site: <http://www.beyondintractability.org>

COUNCIL OF EUROPE, official web site: <http://www.coe.int>; <http://www.eycb.coe.int>

COURT OF AUDIT OF THE REPUBLIC OF SLOVENIA, official web site: <http://www.rs-rs.si>

ELECTORAL RESOURCES, official web site: <http://www.electoralresources.org>

IDEA INTERNATIONAL, official web site: <http://www.idea.int>

INTER-PARLIAMENTARY UNION, official web site: <http://www.ipu.org>

MACEDONIAN NGO "MOST", official web site: <http://www.most.org.mk>

MACEDONIAN HELSINKI COMMITTEE, official web site: <http://www.mhc.org.mk>

OFFICE OF HIGH COMMISSIONER OF HUMAN RIGHT, official web site: <http://www.ohchr.org>

OSCE/ODIHR, official web sites: <http://www.osce.org>; <http://www.osce.org/odihr>

OSCE Research Centre CORE, official web site: <http://www.core-hamburg.de>

STATE ELECTORAL COMMISSION OF THE R. MACEDONIA, official web site: <http:// www.sec.mk>

STATE ELECTORAL COMMISSION OF THE R. SLOVENIA, official web site: <http://www.dvk.gov.si>

UN, official web site: <http://www.un.org>

Printed by Books on Demand GmbH, Norderstedt / Germany